JAEPL, Vol. 30, 2025

JAEPL

The Assembly for Expanded Perspectives on Learning (AEPL), an official assembly of the National Council of Teachers of English, is open to all those interested in extending the frontiers of teaching and learning beyond the traditional disciplines and methodologies.

The purposes of AEPL are to provide a common ground for theorists, researchers, and practitioners to explore innovative ideas; to participate in relevant programs and projects; to integrate these efforts with others in related disciplines; to keep abreast of activities along these lines of inquiry; and to promote scholarship on and publication of these activities.

The *Journal of the Assembly for Expanded Perspectives on Learning, JAEPL*, also provides a forum to encourage research, theory, and classroom practices involving expanded concepts of language. It contributes to a sense of community in which scholars and educators from pre-school through the university exchange points of view and boundary-pushing approaches to teaching and learning. *JAEPL* is especially interested in helping those teachers who experiment with new strategies for learning to share their practices and confirm their validity through publication in professional journals.

Topics of interest include but are not limited to:

- Aesthetic, emotional & moral intelligences
- Learning archetypes
- Kinesthetic knowledge & body wisdom
- Ethic of care in education
- Creativity & innovation
- Pedagogies of healing
- Holistic learning
- Humanistic & transpersonal psychology
- Environmentalism and post-humanism
- (Meta)Cognition
- Imaging & visual thinking
- Intuition & felt sense theory
- Meditation & pedagogical uses of silence
- Narration as knowledge
- Reflective teaching
- Spirituality
- New applications of writing & rhetoric
- Memory & transference
- Multimodality
- Social justice

Membership in AEPL is $45. Contact Jonathan Marine, AEPL, Membership Chair, email: jmarine@gmu.edu. Membership includes current year's issue of *JAEPL*.

Send submissions, address changes, and single hardcopy requests to Wendy Ryden, Editor, *JAEPL*, email: wendy.ryden@liu.edu. Address letters to the editors and all other editorial correspondence to Wendy Ryden (wendy.ryden@liu.edu).

AEPL website: www.aepl.org
Back issues of *JAEPL*: http://trace.tennessee.edu/jaepl/
Blog: https://aeplblog.wordpress.com/
Visit Facebook at **Assembly for Expanded Perspectives on Learning**
Production of *JAEPL* is managed by Parlor Press, https://parlorpress.com.

Assembly for Expanded Perspectives on Learning

Executive Board Chair	Nate Mickelson, New York University
Associate Chair	Rebecca A. Powell, University of Southern Mississippi
Secretary	Liz DeBetta
Treasurer/Membership Chair	Jonathan Marine, Stephen F. Austin State University
CCC Standing Group Liaisons	RAsheda Young, Rutgers University
	Liz DeBetta
TRACE Website	Elizabeth DeGeorge, University of Tennessee, Knoxville
AEPL Website	Daniel J. Weinstein, Indiana University of Pennsylvania
Advisory Board	Sheridan Blau, Teachers College, Columbia University
	Alice G. Brand, SUNY College at Brockport
	John Creger, American High School, Freemont, CA
	Libby Falk Jones, Berea College
	Richard L. Graves, Auburn University, Emeritus
	Doug Hesse, University of Denver
	Laurence Musgrove, Angelo State University
	Nel Noddings, Stanford University
	Sondra Perl, Lehman College, CUNY
	Kurt Spellmeyer, Rutgers University
	Charles Suhor, NCTE
	Joonna Trapp, Emory University
	Jane Tompkins, University of Illinois at Chicago
	Candace Walworth, Naropa University
Founding Members	Alice G. Brand, SUNY College at Brockport
	Richard L. Graves, Auburn University, Emeritus
	Charles Suhor, NCTE
Membership Contact	Jonathan Marine, Stephen F. Austin State University
JAEPL Editor	Wendy Ryden, Long Island University
Assistant and In-Coming Editor	Jonathan Marine, Stephen F. Austin State University

JAEPL is a non-profit journal published yearly by the Assembly for Expanded Perspectives on Learning with support from TRACE at University of Tennessee, Knoxville. Back issues are archived at: http://trace.tennessee.edu/jaepl/.

JAEPL gratefully acknowledges this support as well as that of its manuscript reviewers for their expertise and generosity:

T. J. Geiger, Texas Tech University
Clancy Ratliff, University of Louisiana at Lafayette
Kevin Roozen, University of Central Florida

Donna Strickland, University of Missouri-Columbia
Dan Weinstein, Indiana University of Pennsylvania

JAEPL

The Journal of the Assembly for Expanded Perspectives on Learning

Editor
Wendy Ryden
Long Island University

"Moffett's Corner" Editors
Stephen K. Lafer
University of Nevada Reno

Jonathan M. Marine
Stephen F. Austin State University

Assistant Editor
Jonathan M. Marine
Stephen F. Austin State University

Book Review Editor
Curtis Porter
Indiana University of Pennsylvania

Copyright © 2025
by the Assembly for Expanded Perspectives on Learning
All rights reserved

(ISSN 1085-4630)

An affiliate of the National Council of Teachers of English
Member of the NCTE Information Exchange Agreement
Member of the Council of Editors of Learned Journals
Indexed with MLA Bibliography
Website: www.aepl.org
Blog: https://aeplblog.wordpress.com/
Visit Facebook at **Assembly for Expanded Perspectives on Learning**
Back issues available open access at: http://trace.tennessee.edu/jaepl/

Volume 30 • 2025

Contents

The End of Something—or Not ... 1
Wendy Ryden

Moffett's Corner

James Moffett's Basic Principles ... 4
Stephen Lafer and Jonathan Marine

Writing Without Peter: Reflections on Peter Elbow and His Legacy

Peter Elbow the Philosopher ... 9
Irene Papoulis

"Narrative Medicine Saved My Life": Writing Is a Verb as Well as a Noun ... 15
Marian Mesrobian MacCurdy and Sarah Robinson

Essays

Mindful Administration: Toward a Theory of Academic Leadership We Can Live With ... 32
Sue Doe and Janelle Adsit

Connecting

Bringing Mindfulness into First-Year Composition ... 57
Matthew Lemas

A View from the Conference
Writing Our Spiritual Autobiographies

My Dad's Playful God ... 61
Bhushan Aryal

Books: My Paths to Spirituality ... 63
Beverly Brannan

Tale of an Italian American Buddhist ... 64
Geraldine DeLuca

On Welcome ... 66
Nate Mickelson

An Anti-Spiritual Autobiography ... 68
Laurence Musgrove

Divinity in Nature: Peace in Presence ... 69
Kristin Rajan

Resiliency vs. Uncertainty 71
Adrian Matt Zytkoskee

Books

Is it Just Me? 75
Curt Porter

Cope, Emily M. *Evangelical Writing in a Secular Imaginary: The Academic Writing of Christian Undergraduates at a Public University* 78
Kelly Morgan Sauskojus

Poetter, Thomas S. *Curriculum Fragments: A Currere Journey Through Life Processes* 82
Joseph Wiederhold

Williams, Bronwyn T. *Literacies in Times of Disruption: Living and Learning During a Pandemic* 86
Ashna Singh

Contributors to JAEPL, Vol. 30 89

The End of Something—or Not

Wendy Ryden

When I heard of Peter Elbow's death this past year, I felt that poignancy we experience when the icons of our age depart. Truly, we were not just saying goodbye to Peter the individual but something even more: an era. As a teacher "raised" on the composition theories Peter championed, I felt my life contextualized, a moment in time. I started asking questions like, what's changed since I began my academic journey? What's been for the better? What's not? Perhaps my wonderings are inflected by watching Netflix's fascinating adaptation of Giuseppe Tomasi di Lampedusa's *Il Gattopardo*, a testament to a crumbling Sicilian aristocracy, whose grace was irremediably flawed by inherent waste and oppression—and an emerging new order of equitable possibility, marred by short-sighted human greed, opportunism, and shallow ambition. Maybe, too, the milieu that birthed Peter's ideas are from a past whose beauty and authenticity were at the expense of naivete about privilege, contexts, and stringent realities. Maybe the path of our profession is on a progressive trajectory, but maybe we are also awash in positivist illusions about how far we have come, or are too under attack by greater revanchist forces to have the effectiveness we might wish. Have we lost more than we gained in our embrace of inevitable technologies and institutional jargons that can obfuscate the genuine feelings upon which human empathy and ethical action depend? And I can't help looking at our current America as a report card on educators' efforts: what have we wrought?

If it's fair to be wary of nostalgia when looking at the past, then we should be equally wary of the present's band wagons. I know I have succumbed to both these traps at various times. In Lampedusa's novel about a country's changing allegiances, the author proposes the (in)famous assertion that in order to keep everything the same, everything will have to change. In my own bowdlerizing of the sentiment, I turn it into a question: will everything change only to stay the same? That is not necessarily an expression of hopeless futility, although it could be. But perhaps the good of the past can surface alongside the good of the present. If there were shortcomings in Peter's contribution, I still believe so much of what he promoted is indispensable, maybe now more than ever, especially if we build upon it, rather than against it.

Maybe nostalgia is merely yesterday's band wagon. I do indeed remember feeling a kind of pity, even condescension, for teachers who were "unenlightened" about the perspectives that Peter and others offered us, but of course his influence spread far and wide, especially through WAC and other interdisciplinary efforts. As for myself, I simply can't imagine what my own life as a teacher or scholar would have looked like without Peter's work. Like many, I first encountered *Writing without Teachers* in my required teaching practicum as a graduate student, and it formed the basis of my orientation towards higher education from that point on, even when I wasn't consciously thinking about it. As the years passed, many other welcome and important perspectives also shaped—and rocked—my academic life and pedagogy, but Peter's belief that you have to write the "wrong" words first in order to get to the "right" ones remains foundational. I miss the days when it seemed so much easier to write using only pen and paper in class, since it was all we had, scribbling away together, in a way that seemed to inspire a common vulnerability, no laptop to hide behind or scroll through, students more forthcoming in reading their work aloud and sharing thoughts. No doubt I am romanticizing, like the expressivists were often accused of doing, but I plan on holding onto those sweet memories.

Peter was a particularly important personage for AEPL—he attended and keynoted our annual conferences, working side by side with participants, playing his viola at evening gatherings, setting his cafeteria tray down with the rest of us at breakfast after early morning walks at the Y camp in the Rockies. At the time of his death, he was the Chair of our Advisory Board. So for our members and readers of this journal, it is especially important that we mark our farewell to him and, I think, take joy in all we carry forward with us. In "Peter Elbow the Philosopher," we are so very lucky to have Irene Papoulis, past AEPL Chair, reflect on how her friendship with Peter gave her a distinctive insight into who he was and what he achieved—and how we are all the better for it. She assures us that whether we realize it or not, Peter's work remains influential and relevant in the legacy he bequeathed. I agree wholeheartedly, and Marian MacCurdy and Sarah Robinson's essay, "'Narrative Medicine Saved My Life': Writing Is a Verb as Well as a Noun," is a great illustration of how Peter's wisdom took trajectories that perhaps he wouldn't even have imagined. Marian, who is one of the pioneers of the writing and healing movement, tells us how meeting Peter and reading his work set her upon a path that still helps students, such as her co-author Sarah, learn about the power of authentic writing to transform lives. Indeed, all the work in this issue seems to assure us that Peter's academic lineage *will* continue—and in marvelous ways.

And so will *JAEPL*'s. The wonderful contributions in this landmark issue (our 30th!) assure us that the heart and mind, perhaps the soul, too, continue to mean something to many of us who value teaching and learning, whether it is in the classroom, our administrative work, or our scholarship, all of which seems harder than ever to execute in a world increasingly averse to the value of meaningful education. But regardless of what might change or stay the same in higher education and the world at large, many people still hunger for and produce the kind of work for which *JAEPL* has always provided a home. Thus, it is with a certain wistful fatigue but also optimism that, with this issue, I finish my stint as editor to make room for our in-coming editor, Jonathan M. Marine, who is serving as assistant editor for *JAEPL* 30. I am grateful for all the many, many intelligent, kind, thoughtful, insightful, loving, and generous people who have worked with me over the last six years, especially contributors, reviewers, past editors, AEPL board members, and the personnel at Parlor Press and TRACE. I am grateful for their invaluable help and encouragement; I am grateful for all they have taught me. I have no doubt that our beloved journal will flourish under its new editor, and I wish him great success in carrying on its evolving yet rooted traditions. Welcome, Jonathan. Let the expanded perspectives live on!

MOFFETT'S CORNER

James Moffett's Basic Principles

Stephen Lafer and Jonathan Marine

Jonathan

The tricky part about trying to distill James Moffett's basic principles is that there are so many of them. In literature, the "major" poets are separated form the "minor" for a number of reasons, but one critical criteria is development; major poets have to *develop* across the span of their careers, either writing in new forms, or about and with new ideas or themes. Suffice to say, Moffett developed a great deal across his career, from a focus on pedagogy to a focus on spirituality and mindfulness along with increasing consideration of educational assessment and policy. Of course, I'm overgeneralizing here; grasping at "a strategic gain in concept," and Moffett's career and interests were far more complicated, interrelated, and kinetic than this paltry encapsulation can offer (Moffett, *Discourse* v). However, my point is that a discussion of his core principles threatens another overgeneralization; Moffett means different things in different contexts to different types of people, and moreover and more importantly, he has *many* core principles.

To me, there is one core idea which fundamentally conveys across his oeuvre. However, first, it's important to remember that Moffett offered one of the only fully formed L1 language learning theories in our field by centering on the concept of abstraction because he believed it was one of the only analytic and theoretical constructs capable of conveying *across all languages*. That's a shockingly ambitious notion, but one that Moffett was able to pare down to a relatively parsimonious schema. He proposed a dual-axis model of discourse splayed across two axes of increasing abstractive distance. The longitudinal axis plots the I-you spectrum, or the distance between speaker/writer and listener/reader. Starting with reflection, defined as "intrapersonal communication between two parts of one nervous system," onto conversation ("two people in vocal range"), correspondence ("interpersonal communication between remote individuals"), and "publication" ("impersonal communication to a large anonymous group, extended over space or time') (Moffett, *Discourse* 33). Conversely, the latitudinal axis plots the I-it spectrum between the speaker/writer and their subject, from what is happening (describing/recording), to what happened (reporting/narrating), to what happens (generalizing), to what may, could, or should happen (arguing/theorizing).

what is happening—drama—recording
what happened—narrative—reporting
what happens—exposition—generalizing
what may happen—logical argumentation

Moffett's I-It Spectrum

Reflection   Intrapersonal communication between two parts of one nervous system

Conversation   Interpresonal communication between two people in vocal range.

Correspondence Interpersonal communication between remote individuals or small groups with some personal knowledge of each other.

Publication   Impersonal communication to a large anonymous group extended over space and/or time.

Moffett's I-You Spectrum

For English, Language Arts, and Writing teachers, Moffett's discourse schema provides not only a way of translating all of these different forms of communication into an almost limitless amount of different ways of writing (and it's worth remembering how narrow and provincial the range of classroom writing was in the 1950s and 60s), but also a way of overlaying types of thought onto types of writing that encourage us to think about the loss of fidelity that transpires as we process raw experience into thought and then express it to others. As Moffett puts it, "to abstract is to trade a loss of reality for a gain in control" (Moffett, *Discourse* 23). And Moffett's many pedagogical efforts to design writing and language arts curriculum (including 1973's *Interaction*, four editions of *Student-Centered Language Arts*, and the four volumes of *Active Voice*) in essence parlay varying transmissions across these levels of abstraction with and against one another in order to demonstrate and inspire in readers further awareness of the abstractive spectrum which he contends undergirds all human communication. Whether that's first recording an experience as it happens and later turning it into a historical account, work of fiction, or drama (going from *what is happening* to *what happened* or *what may well or could happen*) OR rewriting a reflection as a letter to another person or group of people (going from reflection to correspondence or publication), Moffett's discourse schema allows us all to see the many different ways communication takes place and how they interact with, bind to, and incarnate one another.

In conversations with colleagues, when the notion of "student-centered" arises, in my experience it often devolves into trite discussions of student choice; advocating for letting learners do, read, or write what they want in the classroom (something that is more Montessorian than Moffettian, to my mind). Sometimes, a daring Brahmin will even go so far as to suggest (often in a tone that indicates they believe they've discovered a new element on the periodic table) that student writing be *authentic*; that they write as they do in the real world (which, again, to me, has more to do with Peter Elbow or even Kenneth Bruffee than Moffett). It's not that these notions don't align with the student-centered, or that Moffett didn't consider them or value them or account for them in his ideas and theories. However, what strikes me as the core tenant of student-centerdness which runs throughout all of Moffett's work is the connection across his abstractive scales *back* from any form of writing *to* our own experience.

To Moffett, all language is egocentric; bore out of the understandings, or generalizations, which our experience has exteriorized for us. Accordingly, growth and development are hinged on decreasing egocentrism; "awareness that meaning resides in minds, not in words, and that different people may see the same things differently, verbalize the same ideas differently, and interpret the same words differently" (Moffett, *Detecting* 20). To be student centered presumes student choice much as it presumes authentic discourse (what would be the point of writing inauthentic discourse, exactly?), but it also goes beyond those elements to the invaluable realization that we only understand the world around us *through* our own experiences, and in that way, Moffett's core principle of student-centeredness helps us to bind thought to language as anchored in the understandings wrought from our own experience; to never lose sight of ourselves in the vast, monochromatic mist of abstraction which language threatens to foment all around us. "To see a leaf is not to incorporate it, nor literally to transform it (the leaf remains the same), but rather to create in our body a representation of it that is structurally similar to it" (Moffett, *Discourse* 20). Moffett's core principle of student-centered learning is about letting student's experience become the sextant with which they navigate the universe of discourse, and beyond.

Steve

Abstraction, as Moffett argues, is ever-present in how we make sense of the world. And as Jonathan reminds us, what we know is always filtered through our own perceptions, generalizations, and sense of self. In this way, becoming a literate citizen requires an awareness of both our own perceptual filters and an ability to engage with others' perspectives. For Moffett, education is not merely about transmitting knowledge but about exploring the conditions that make understanding possible. As a life-long educator, I've long believed that a good education is rooted in helping students learn to measure distance—between people, the different ideas we may have, and between the expression of those ideas and meaning.

Jonathan aptly outlines Moffett's discourse schema, his two-axis model charting abstraction in relation to audience (from intrapersonal to public) and subject (from recording to theorizing). This model is more than a taxonomy, it's a map for navigating language and experience. It urges us to attend not just to what we say, but to the layers of distance (personal, temporal, conceptual) that shape how meaning is made.

In my own teaching, I've found Moffett's ideas most powerful when enacted in project-based classrooms; that is, spaces where students move among rhetorical roles and test their ideas in real exchanges. For instance, dramatic performances invite students into the "what is happening now" mode of discourse. Theater also demands empathy and perspective-taking. It forces students to see how thoughts become actions that shape character, drive conflict, and advance the plot. This kind of active, multimodal engagement fosters dialogic critical thinking in the Vygotskian sense: thinking about thinking through the voices and experiences of others.[1]

Once students have experienced the immediacy of drama, they can begin to shift into narration by reporting *what has happened*. This introduces distance and abstraction. Reporting requires memory, reflection, and the ability to represent reality from a position of separation. This space can also help students see the difference between being present in a moment and recalling it; between experiencing something and communicating it effectively.

Generalizing, the next level of abstraction, asks students to spot patterns and theorize beyond individual cases. This is where students learn to distinguish strong from weak claims, test ideas against evidence, and refine their grasp of what holds across contexts. And this type of thinking is absolutely essential for civic reasoning and decision-making. A classroom organized to facilitate generalization *must* allow students to compare texts, perspectives, and experiences, and in doing so it must foster an environment where patterns can emerge and be discussed.

Theory-making, the apex of Moffett's schema, is about imagining what could be. To theorize is to build frameworks that extend beyond what is or even what has been. It is where abstraction reaches its full potential. Theory, grounded in

---

1. It should come as no surprise to readers that Moffett draws heavily upon Vygotsky (as well as many other notable thinkers of his era, including Piaget and Bruner). Some examples of comments on Vygotsky by Moffett can be found on page 17 and 64 of *Teaching the Universe of Discourse* (1968, 1983).

generalizations tested against experience and evidence, is the foundation for invention and creativity. Whether in fiction, social analysis, or scientific hypotheses, theorizing enables students to propose futures, anticipate outcomes, and build new possibilities.

Moffett's schema doesn't just describe how communication works, but gives students a framework for participating meaningfully in discourse communities. And that requires educators to build classrooms where students both climb *and* descend the ladder of abstraction. That ladder, in turn, depends on language-rich environments. That is, places where students are constantly composing and comprehending with real audiences and real stakes.

To support this kind of development, instruction must be dialogic. Moffett's model thrives when students are immersed in purposeful activity: writing letters, scripting plays, producing podcasts, staging debates, and composing essays. The classroom becomes a space for experimentation, collaboration, and reflection. And the teacher's role shifts from dispenser of content to architect of experience. Teachers can and some be engaged in designing conditions where thought and language grow together.

What unites all of these modes of discourse is the idea that literacy is not about finding the right answer, but about navigating the distance between the self, the other, and the world. Students need classrooms where they climb (and descend) Moffett's ladder of abstraction with purpose, engage in inquiry, and produce language that matters because it is rooted in experience. The aim is not to simplify, but to help students manage complexity and locate themselves within it.

As Jonathan notes, Moffett's notion of student-centeredness is often reduced to discussions of choice or authenticity. But at its core, it's about epistemology. It's about recognizing that knowledge begins in the self, and that growth depends on seeing through the eyes of others. This is not simply a method, it is an ethical orientation, and one that is as important in today's socio-political climate as ever. To be student-centered in Moffett's sense is to respect that all understanding begins in experience, and that the goal of education is not the abandonment of egocentrism but the mindful movement beyond it.

In future columns, I hope to explore how Moffett's model can inform classroom design through discussion of class assignments and environments that cultivate abstraction, empathy, and critical thought. Writing, literacy, and disciplinary learning can, and should, be interwoven into a pedagogy rooted in abstraction and student agency. For now, it's enough to say that Moffett gives us a theory of literacy that is also a theory of humanity. And in this moment, we need both.

WRITING WITHOUT PETER: REFLECTIONS ON PETER ELBOW AND HIS LEGACY

Peter Elbow the Philosopher

Irene Papoulis

On the occasion of Peter Elbow's passing, we read many tributes and praises commemorating him and the foundational contributions he made to the multi-faceted field of writing studies. But as we know, even as Peter's ideas were lauded and embraced, they were also questioned by many, including other renowned members of our profession.

I once asked Peter how he most wanted to be seen in the academic world, and he said, "as a philosopher." Many in our field might be surprised by that. Since Peter wrote about the messy, emotional side of what happens when we write, and since he wrote about feelings, including his own, and listening without speaking, and Rogerian rhetoric, many seemed to view him as a giant neon sign beaming TOUCHY-FEELY. That made them trap him in a box and run away, eschewing what they might have deemed his wacky, and ultimately unserious, worldview. Their dismissiveness hurt him more than most people knew.

My friendship with Peter began through something called Re-evaluation Counseling, also known as Co-Counseling or just "RC." It's a peer-to-peer therapy that people learn about mostly by word of mouth. They take a class in the method and then meet outside of class to "counsel" each other.

It is not a vetted practice. But back in the eighties, when I was a graduate student in English at Stony Brook University and had never heard of Peter, a friend talked me into going to an RC class. Emotions, the teacher told our incoming group of recruits, often prevent us from thinking clearly; she was going to teach us how to "discharge" those emotions with the help of others. There was nothing wrong with emotions in themselves, she added—in fact, respecting them was crucial in the process we would learn for "counseling:" getting the other person to express their emotions in order to "discharge" them. Once we learned how to do that we would meet in pairs, usually with people who were separate from our regular lives, decide on a time window, divide that time in half and, say we meet for an hour, you "counsel" me for the first thirty minutes, then we switch and I do the same for you. If we met someone for the first time in the class, we weren't allowed to socialize with them outside of class or counseling.

"Counseling" was an intriguing process to me at the time, and I participated in it for a couple of years. It taught me to ask good questions, listen carefully, and maybe say back the person's words, or ask them to dig into their emotional valences by repeating specific phrases they had spoken. I was slightly uncomfortable about the fact that we did all this without oversight from a "real" therapist, but I found it very interesting to establish close connections with strangers, separate from the rest of our lives, by getting each other to laugh, cry, and shake.

Meanwhile, over in the real world I was beginning my dissertation and teaching various sections of first-year composition. One day, I learned that Peter Elbow was going to become the director of Stony Brook's writing program. Who? I didn't know, but got his book, *Writing Without Teachers*, and became intrigued.

We graduate students had our first meeting with Peter in a classroom, and his first move was to insist that we move the desks from their rows into a big circle. What? Even in "discussion" classes, we hadn't done that unless we had a seminar table. Then he got us to freewrite. What? "This is not to share, just write whatever comes, for yourself, the only rule is that you don't stop. Repeat, 'no, no, no,' if you want, but keep the pen moving." What? But I'm writing garbage!

No matter. And of course, by now, hundreds of thousands of people have had similar introductions to the pleasures of freewriting, and countless words have been written, stemming from *Writing without Teachers*, about the usefulness of private freewriting and its "garbage." I quickly became a convert to Peter's methods, both as a teacher and as a writer.

And one day, I picked up the phone, and it was Peter. "I see that you're in RC," I was surprised to hear him say, "would you like to meet for co-counseling?" Wow—in those pre-internet days, I hadn't known I was in any kind of database. But hey, counsel with the program chair? "Ok, sure!"

Private meetings for "counseling" between a program director and a graduate student might sound creepy or suspect in this post #metoo era, and if that phone conversation had happened today I probably would have hesitated quite a bit, wondering about Peter's intentions as a 48-year old professor counseling with a 28-year old graduate student. But back then, I saw the invitation simply as an interesting opportunity, which it turned out to be. I did feel a bit awkward in our sessions at first, probably curating my feelings in order to appear more dignified than I knew I was. That wasn't the best way for me to "discharge" my real feelings, but Peter's open, non-judgmental spirit helped me come to think of myself as his equal partner when it came to counseling, and we both took the work seriously—it wasn't creepy at all.

A rule of RC is that everything in a session is confidential, but I can say that Peter and I learned quite a bit about each other's emotions. That felt somewhat strange to me when I saw him in the halls of the English building; it put us outside the usual norms of director/student interaction. But I appreciated the fact that both Peter and I were comfortable with our resistance to those norms, in the name of personal growth. We were both drawn to RC for its outsider-ness, I'd say, before going on to become captivated by the power of its basic tenets.

I never took a class with Peter, since I was done with coursework by then, but I attended various writing and reading groups he led, and I read all his writings. As a result of that study, my teaching improved dramatically.

After I left Stony Brook, and RC, in 1986, Peter and I stayed in touch as friends, colleagues, and later participants in a longtime three-person writing group with our friend Don Jones. Although we no longer "counseled," our friendship was fueled by the way we had gotten to know each other.

A few years into my first teaching job, at the University of California, Santa Barbara, I was part of a summer institute for teachers sponsored by SCWRIP, Southern California's branch of the National Writing Project. Peter was an invited speaker, and the teachers were excited to meet him and see what he was like in person. Someone he loved had recently died, and he told me before his talk that he was feeling emotionally raw. Soon after he somewhat shakily began his presentation, sitting at a desk at the front of the crowded room, he suddenly stopped and looked into the audience with his characteristic quizzical squint.

"Irene," he said, "would you mind coming up here as I give my talk?" Who me? Yes. I stood up and walked awkwardly to the front of the room. He said, "would you hold my hand as I give the lecture?" Um, okay. I pulled up a chair. Peter took my hand and proceeded. As I sat up there, I felt a mixture of emotions: embarrassment, as I imagined people thinking, "what is *she* doing up there?"; pride, since I was flattered to be recognized as someone Peter would single out for comfort; and a little bit of judgmentalism: how could he not be able to give the lecture *by himself*?

I know enough to realize that that latter feeling was about me, not him. Ironically, given my theoretical belief in the importance of vulnerability, part of me felt that Peter's blatant example of openness in the context of a lecture was somehow inappropriate, a violation of the unspoken academic code of calm rationality. In other words, he scared me by being so open about his emotions, and that fear expressed itself in me as secret criticism of him.

Exploring that fear of mine gives me insight, I think, into the attitudes of so many people in our field of Rhet/Comp who judge Peter harshly, assuming that his association with "feelings" encourages students to "contemplate their navels" and thus be prevented from critiquing their own subjective stances, and/or engaging with the rigors of analytic thinking and writing in the academy. Peter had responses to that false assumption (see all of his writings) but many people didn't take the time to explore those. Could their judgement at times have been a result of their ambivalences about their own vulnerability? Were they, in a sense, scared of the desire to, say, admit to wanting someone to hold their hand in an academic setting when they were feeling fragile?

Those of us who were active in the field in the 1980s and 90s remember the chasm that opened up between "expressivists" and "social constructionists."

Most of us probably took a side and fought to defend it against the other side. I myself was always comfortable on the expressivist side, but I can tell you that Peter himself chafed against the idea of being called an expressivist. He thought it was unfair and reductive, and he hated the bin it threw him into, one that was filled with all the emoters and none of the sophisticated thinkers. Yes, he believed in emotional risks and self-investigations. But—along with most so-called expressivists— he *never* left it there. He always took it to, "and what can my emotions help me learn about other people, other ideas, that are different from mine?" He always advocated, and lived, the practice of embracing the contraries—allowing ourselves to move between extremes in order to get to truer insights, and then keep moving further, to more contradictions, more questioning, and more insights into ourselves as well as others.

Peter *was* a philosopher, one who began with a bodily refusal to view the world of ideas as independent of the world of lived feelings. He was radical, in the sense that he truly, not just in theory, wanted everyone in every room to have a voice and be able to speak. He did everything he could, in his life and teaching as well as his writing, to make that happen. He loved jokes, yes, but he was dead serious about ideas. Faced with peoples' characterization of him as lightweight, he often said, in frustration, something like, "I'm not touchy-feely, well maybe I am, but I'm also the other side more."

His phrase "embracing contraries," also the title of one of his collections of essays, describes his way of being in the world. Things are one way, but in fact they're also the opposite. It's useful to *believe* people, but *doubting*, he always said, is a crucial skill, and of course, is fundamental to the academic world. Writing is cerebral, but it's also emotional. Teachers are friendly and nice, but we're also authorities who judge and then wield grades. I love the title of his essay (printed in *Embracing Contraries*) about the latter paradox, which he called "The Pedagogy of the Bamboozled:" Do what you want, teachers say, but wait, not *that*!

To Peter, embracing the contraries never meant smushing them together, as some people may have assumed. It meant letting them exist as they are, in a way that allows us to see them more clearly. Our field has embraced "both/and" these days, which I'd say Peter would appreciate, but he'd also caution us not to use that stance to give up too quickly on particularities.

I've been thinking about the relationship between Peter's academic work and a fundamental rule of RC counseling: when someone is telling their story, and feeling its emotions, you should step out of the way and listen. Don't tell them about the time you felt the same way; don't give them advice; just listen. There is a lot of freedom in that principle, which leads the person being counseled to the beautiful feeling of being heard and accepted, no matter what. That's the essence of Peter's teaching, I'd say: Let everyone have a voice in the room; respect all voices; always listen to outsiders. So simple, and yet so vexed.

But you *can't* respect all voices. You *have* to make judgements about them. Our vantage points limit us. Peter, as many people pointed out, was a privileged white man, not fully able to appreciate the kinds of pressures he never had to deal with. That's true, and if Peter were here, he would want to continue discussing and writing about the ramifications of that. He loved to pull at the nuances of everything, and he had an impressive ability to consider ideas from many angles. Yes, it's true, he'd say, but the opposite can be true too, no? Argue *for* your position, he liked to advise, not against. Maybe you'll learn something, and it will probably make you more convincing to the other side. The Believing Game, as he conceived it, never meant just belief! It meant taking time to embody the other side. "What would it mean," he'd ask, "to believe what people on the other side believe. Can you imagine yourself into their perspective?" That process insists that we take responsibility for our whole-body experience, not just our intellect. It doesn't mean *staying* in the other perspective, nor flipping over to their side. No, it can help us to understand the foundations of our own perspectives more deeply, even as we become more open to adjusting them. And it certainly helps us to engage with the other side more productively.

I think it's important for our field that we continue to explore and honor Peter's ideas and their ramifications for bodily, not just intellectual, experience. Our commitment to social justice could falter if we don't.

At the 2025 4Cs conference, I went to a large, very popular ballroom session on responding to writing. Panelists talked about reflective writing, process letters, collaborations in peer review, and ungrading, and they didn't mention Peter Elbow's name once, even in their lists of references. I stood up to point that out, and one of the panelists quickly said something like, "oh yes, he wrote about responding back in the day."

Okay, and fortunately, many of the panel's ideas did grow out of work that Peter did for decades. That made me think about how much our field continues to be shaped by his thinking, even for those who don't know, or associate themselves with, his name. His ideas about freewriting and pedagogy, as well as voice, language, assessment, student-centered classrooms, responding to writing, and the academic subject of English are indelibly embedded in the teaching of college and high school writing everywhere. Does it matter that his name is getting lost in the overflowing heap of forgotten, albeit influential, "expressivists"?

Of course, Peter did also feel the love from many in our field and beyond, including those of us affiliated with AEPL and *JAEPL*. He got countless recognitions and awards, and wherever he went, strangers came up to thank him for his work. He knew that he had a long-lasting influence on the way thousands and thousands of people teach, talk, and write.

There's so much more to say about you, Peter, and about your impact on our field, and on anyone who knew you personally, or saw you do one of your very quirky, funny, rambling, digressing, unforgettable, powerful, deep, and thoroughly unique lectures, many of which were at 4C's conferences. Most who heard you lecture said they'd never seen anything like it before, nor since.

In our quirkiness is our power, you taught us, and also in our feelings, our listenings, and our openness. You lived your ideas, and there were always more angles, questions, asides, and sinews to them. Your insistence that each of us strive to be our own selves is so powerful, and is what the world needs. Your impact on writers, on teachers, on friends, on our field of writing studies, on the academy, and on the world, is vast, and when you let yourself really feel that, I know it made you very happy.

"Narrative Medicine Saved My Life":
Writing Is a Verb as Well as a Noun

Marian Mesrobian MacCurdy and Sarah Robinson

The exchanging of stories isn't fun or desirable. It's something essential to our well-being."

—Kazuo Ishiguro

Dedicated to Professor Peter Elbow
4/14/1935 – 2/6/2025

I, Marian, began my career as a graduate student in medieval literature who had a teaching assistantship to fund her degree. As a graduate student I lived in a world that saw writing as a noun, something done and finished, not as a verb, a process that shows us a world that is as ever-changing as we are. But as a writing teacher I found myself sliding into the world that writers inhabit, and I realized that I was not only earning a degree but finding a new profession.

I attended a conference at Penn State and heard, then met, Professor Peter Elbow. I learned then that what I had been sensing in my relationships with my students was true: we don't teach subjects; we teach students. We are taught that if you can't say it, you don't know it. But readers say this; writers don't. We can trust language to speak for us, for our deeper selves, but that's hard when language is only seen as something we are judged by. Peter and I spoke a few times after that before he retired from UMass Amherst and moved west where he lived until his recent death. The world has lost a great teacher whose brilliance and humanity has led the way for many of us. His work highlights a sea change in writing pedagogy that will continue to affect the profession for years to come.

Soon after, I was hired to teach in the Department of Writing at Ithaca College. A few years later as department chair I had the chance to explore with our faculty the practice of writing from many different lenses, as we designed a major. Where, we asked, is the student in what we teach and the stories they would like to tell, the stories of adventures or those of loss or other perils? Then I experienced one of those perils myself—the death of my husband and the challenge of raising two young children alone—and my grief gave my students permission to tell the truth, to me, to themselves, and to each other. As Lucille Clifton once said to a room full of educators at a conference, "Every child looking at you has faced something you could not bear."

In this essay Sarah, a young student in my class on her voyage into writing and healing, and I, a veteran teacher and practitioner for whom every writing moment is new, offer an example of a process that can bring clarity, focus, and ultimately peace and understanding to those who need it most—survivors of experiences that separate them from their families, their friends, and even at times themselves. The growth from writing about such experiences begins with learning how to write and goes on to the most important task—learning how to live.

Traumatic memories go through a process of kindling—a kind of etching in the brain which means they are less likely to fade over time the way most ordinary memories do because they tend not to be coherent stories but are intense emotions attached to images and actions, what scientists call "somatosensory impressions," that stick in memory as vibrant, potent images rather than language-based narratives. I give my students this classic example: imagine coming across a snake on a wooded path. The most likely action is sensory: fight, flight, or freeze. We do one of those three things instinctively and fast to protect ourselves. If we had to send our potential responses through the cortex to think about it, the snake could bite us before we ever figured out what to do. So quick action is an important life-saving skill. But since the experience was not logged into the cortex, we have no language around it. We have an engaged amygdala—and that means our emotions are present, and images, sounds, sensations as well—but few thoughts. Thoughts come later, after the crisis is over. But by then we have entrenched feelings to deal with which can keep us from developing a clear cognitive response.

Merely recovering those memories isn't enough to help survivors move past them. They need to be contextualized to allow for communication between left brain verbal thought and right brain emotions and the images, sounds, and smells that generate them. This allows us to connect thoughts and feelings so we can holistically see, hear, smell, even experience the past without being possessed by it. We now can tell our story to ourselves and to others which can provide a certain kind of control over the past—we can choose to tell our story or not, and we can choose the words we use to tell it. The story has been logged into the verbal part of the brain, the part where our history, our stories, reside.

Most important, we can create a sense of self and a voice when we write. Our stories and our genes make up who we are. We can't control our genes—at least not yet—but we can control telling our stories—how to tell them, when to tell them, and most important, *if* to tell them, and to whom. These stories can be joyous and life-giving as well as hard to speak of, yet utterly necessary to find because their effects can appear when we least expect them—when we hear a crash that sounds like the one that totaled our car, when we dream of a dog chasing us that looks and sounds like the one from a childhood fright, or we meet someone who sounds like a beloved family member..

The best way to remember such moments is to know that they are state-specific experiences, and the more details we can remember, the more we can put those experiences in the past if we choose. They are no longer in a holding room waiting for us to deal with them. Writing about them doesn't mean we are free of them, but it can give us a bit of control over that which we cannot control—the past. When we write about such moments, we are pulling up pictures, scenes, images from the non-verbal areas of the brain and using language to locate them within the verbal system where they can be named, labelled, and perhaps put aside when we choose. This is not a get-out-of- jail-free card, of course, but it does provide survivors with some agency—we can decide when and if to write, when to stop writing, and when or if to share our work with others. It becomes our story to tell—or not tell—rather than an experience foisted on us. This process helps writers find the key elements of the experience that help create a vibrant narrative that others may find compelling—and perhaps instructive.

As Peter Elbow and others in the field of narrative writing have understood, writing can unearth truth. When I was run over by a car as a little kid while sliding on a sled on the sidewalk, I was able to get up and walk away so no one was much concerned about me. Miraculously, I had only a small injury to my arm, at least that's what could be seen, but I knew the car ran over me. My terror hid, shown only by the fact that I no longer wanted to hide under beds like I used to. Trauma doesn't disappear; it just hides—often in plain sight--so we have to find it, feel it, speak it, and create a narrative that allows us to move past it. Writing a trauma memoir can make the past the past.

According to current trauma theory, trauma does not result in repression, which involves an effort to hide our difficult experiences, but instead can cause dissociation from traumatic experiences because the resulting images and sensations are too shocking to be integrated and so are never logged into full consciousness in the first place. Instead, those traumatic memories reside in the non-verbal parts of the brain where they can be hidden, unvoiced, not in verbal consciousness. The goal then becomes integration—to find those inchoate memories and make them conscious so they can be spoken about and released. Words can liberate.

Since dissociation is not volitional, survivors do not choose to hide their traumatic memories from themselves, but they can be overwhelmed mentally and emotionally by them as a study discussed by Ellen Barry in *The New York Times* demonstrates. Researchers at Yale and the Icahn School of Medicine at Mount Sinai were looking to find differences between traumatic and non-traumatic memories. Subjects with PTSD listened to recorded narrations of their own memories, some of which were neutral, some sad, and some traumatic. Brain scans conducted during the listening showed clear differences between sad and traumatic memories.

Sad memories showed high engagement of the hippocampus, the part of the brain that organizes and contextualizes memories. Yet when the same people listened to their traumatic memories, such as sexual assaults, fires, and school shootings, the hippocampus was not active. "What it tells us is that the brain is in a different state in the two memories" said Daniela Schiller, neuroscientist and one of the authors of the study. According to Schiller, treatments for PTSD are being investigated to help survivors organize their memories so they can see them as separate from the past because "…the brain doesn't look like it's in a state of memory; it looks like it is in a state of present experience." The authors conclude that "traumatic memories are not experienced as memories as such," but as "fragments of prior events, subjugating the present moment" (qtd. in Barry). This makes the memories harder to put in the past, but that of course, is the goal: to help people move the traumatic memory from an ever-present now to the past, distinct from present experiences.

Non-traumatic memories are stored in networks in the brain, connected to other memories. But trauma memories are often isolated, caught in the non-verbal parts of the brain, making us feel these "internal experiences" are still occurring with danger still present. Current research shows that revisiting the memory with clarity is important to treatment. "You're helping the patient to construct a memory that can be organized and consolidated into the hippocampus," said Dr. Harpaz-Rotem, professor of psychiatry and psychology at Yale University (qtd. in Barry), because "traumatic memories are not remembered; they are re-experienced" (Lanius, qtd. in Barry). The goal then is to transform a chaotic series of trauma images into a more ordinary, if sad, memory and that means "if I can access a memory, I know it is a memory. I know it's not happening to me now." As Bessel van der Kolk wrote, "A patient is victimized by having memories of the event, not by the event itself" (qtd. in Bessel, McFarlane, and Weisaeth 218). This is, of course, cold comfort to the survivor who lives with the impact of the traumatic memory every day.

Ruth Lanius suggested that therapies such as mindfulness can help show that the traumatic experience happened in the past (see Barry). Writing can be a particularly efficacious choice in this regard as it creates a record of one's truth, and the power of such a process and the narrative it produces can be transformational when writers freely choose their topics, which is essential to make sure writers have a sense of personal control.

In what follows, Sarah Robinson, a former student in my course Narrative Medicine: How Writing Can Heal, demonstrates the importance of using writing to bridge the gap between silent trauma and vocal acknowledgment to self and perhaps others. Trauma isolates; language connects. In addition to the beneficial effects of organizing traumatic experience into coherent memory, writing also can show us we are a part of the community, in spite of, and sometimes because of, what has happened to us. In the process we can produce a piece of writing that has the grace of truth and the heart of relief. The following is Sarah's story in her own words:

"It Was Dark"

Sarah Robinson

I came to Dr. MacCurdy's class, "Narrative Medicine: How Writing Can Heal," in the Fall of 2021, as a newly declared English major. I was severely mentally ill, but unaware that I was mentally ill. It's a terrible experience; it's almost dangerous. I look fine and seem fine, but no one could see the storm inside of me, threatening to topple the ship and drown it in its unforgiving seas. I was living with undiagnosed PTSD, a general anxiety disorder, an eating disorder, and a history of depression and suicidal thoughts, all from being raped when I was fourteen. I wrote the following in a journal entry at the beginning of the semester:

> I see you everywhere. I thought you had gone away. Here I was, naively thinking I had gotten rid of all my demons. And there you were, walking past me in the dining hall. Sitting down in the cafeteria with your headphones on, holding the door for me, walking past me with your friends. I double back and take a closer look. It's just someone who looks vaguely like you. It's like seeing a ghost, and I don't believe in ghosts. But their hair is too long, and they're not lanky enough. Hell, you're supposed to be on a different continent. Even the Atlantic Ocean isn't enough distance. Even if you died, it wouldn't be enough distance.

I was raped when I was fourteen in my home by my first boyfriend. We'll call him Adam. I didn't sleep for the first six months after the assault. And when I did fall asleep, as humans are eventually forced to do, it was from emotional exhaustion. I cried so much that I would wake up with completely swollen eyelids. Some days, I couldn't even open my eyes. My parents and my pediatrician thought I had conjunctivitis, and I would get a day here and there off from school. I didn't tell them that the swelling was really from my crying so hard at night I would choke. I slept on tear-soaked pillows. I remember on some of the worst nights I prayed and pleaded with God to make it all stop. I didn't care how it stopped. I didn't care if I died. I just wanted everything to stop.

I was never put in therapy or counseling after the assault, even with my increasingly frequent panic attacks. Then in March 2020 of my senior year of high school I broke down. I almost passed out in my AP Physics class, then was bedridden for three days. As soon as I started to think about doing schoolwork, I would have a panic attack. Therapy wasn't a question then. I knew something was broken.

The therapist diagnosed me with anxiety, nothing severe, just normal teen-aged school anxiety. I "graduated" therapy after a few months. He told me I was healed. I never told him about my assault. That probably would have been helpful information. But he was a him. And I didn't trust hims. At least, I didn't trust this specific him enough with my story. "He wouldn't have understood" is what I told myself. He would've told me it was my fault or that I should've been smarter, better or that I should've stopped it. I heard all those thoughts in an endless loop in my head, so I didn't need one more voice to add to the medley.

For five years, I kept everything behind closed doors. I cried alone, every day. I would blast music in my ears and just allow myself to emote, to feel, to say everything I couldn't, to scream.

I entered Narrative Medicine with the belief that writing could heal as it had been healing me my whole life. Dr. MacCurdy walked into the class on the first day pulling her wheeled computer bag, and had a mask pulled tight around her face with the elastics digging into the sides of her face. There were ten of us in the class, and only a few were English majors. The opening assignment was to write a personal essay, in first person (that was very important), about a traumatic or challenging moment in your life to mirror and experience the practical aspect of the essays we were reading.

In writing my narrative essay I followed the *Writing Cure*'s Exhibit 10.1 in chapter ten of the book. First there is Stage 1: "Individual is remote from feeling. Reported experiences have an impersonal quality. Feelings are avoided and personal involvement is not present in communication" (Lutgendorf and Ullrich 181). I told Professor MacCurdy in my writing autobiography (a get to know you exercise and the first assignment of the semester) that I was raped and that was the beginning of my journey of dealing with trauma. She suggested that might be a topic to write about, if I wished. I refused. I was in Stage 1. I was in fact, angry she suggested that I delve into that again. I felt like it was over and in the past. And to me giving it any more attention was a waste. I wrote one poem a few months prior for a different class and wrote that trauma off as healed. But it was never over for me. I kept re-experiencing the trauma every time I saw someone that looked remotely similar to the abuser. So I decided to write about my step-grandfather's death in an essay titled "Comfort Food." It ended up being less of an essay about my step-grandfather's death but about my complicated relationship with my mother. It was an essay with no central idea and turning it in felt wrong. But I so wanted to avoid the trauma that I chose the easier path.

Reluctantly, after talking with Professor MacCurdy one-on-one, I decided to write about my sexual assault. There was a lot of separation, even blockages, between me and the sexual assault. It was clear in my writing that I had almost no emotional attachment to the event. Similar to chapter three of *The Mind's Eye*, MacCurdy quotes Freyd, "'on an intellectual level, I knew that I had been a victim of incest along with physical and emotional abuse... On an emotional level, I felt numb. When talking about my experiences, it was as though I was speaking about someone totally separate from myself'" (136). I felt an extreme separation between my sexual assault and myself. It was almost like it happened to a completely different girl, and I was no longer that girl. This I can attribute to my mind dissociating during the sexual assault.

I felt so detached from it all that I struggled to grasp at any memory I had. However, his voice rang through my head daily. I wrote an entire piece of writing that was a back-and-forth conversation between myself (now) and Adam. I couldn't hear my voice (the voice of the fourteen-year-old girl who had been raped), but I could hear his voice vividly in my head. In Anne Ruggles Gere's chapter two titled "Whose Voice Is It Anyway?" Gere's professor, Robert Smith, suggested that she "needed speech therapy because [her] voice didn't project." She writes "when I listened to a tape, I was startled. Mine was a soft voice, full of breath and hesitancy. It was my mother's voice" (Gere 26). As Gere recognized her own voice as her mother's, I recognized mine as my rapist's voice. Robert Smith sees Gere's voice as something to be fixed. Gere writes, "Just as Professor Smith would have dismissed my detailed explanation of how I came to have the voice he and I heard on the tape recorder, so we often consider our students' voices separate from the particular family history, significant persons, and events that helped shape them" (27-28). I could not separate my voice as a writer from my sexual assault. I am constantly writing stories of the relationship between good and evil and devils in disguises, because those have been themes of my life not just with my sexual assault. The perpetrator's voice trampling the victim's voice is a common experience among sexual assault survivors. Dr. MacCurdy writes that "sexual abuse survivors have additional challenges: Addressing their inner worlds means confronting a perpetrator who in their minds may still have power over them—a fearsome shadow that can cause everything from writer's block to personality changes" (130). Adam still existed in my head and because of that I felt like I was unable to write about my sexual assault. Just as MacCurdy said, Adam was the cause of my writer's block. I could not isolate my sexual assault from my voice as a writer or from my life story, but I couldn't let Adam trample my voice or that of the fourteen-year-old girl.

For the first real draft, I wrote in detail about how Adam and I started dating. But I refrained from adding any details to it. I went on for four pages about how my friends convinced me to date him and about the first time I met him in the first person. Then when talking about the actual sexual assault I wrote, "then all the stuff happened the weekend my parents were away." That was the most I referenced my sexual assault in the entire draft. I was still in Stage 1 of the *Writing Cure*'s chart. My writing had an "impersonal quality," and my "personal involvement" was excluded from it (Lutgendorf and Ullrich 181).

Between the two drafts, I had a meeting with Professor MacCurdy and found a lot of comfort in it. After our first meeting she told me I should seek professional help. I had been thinking about it for a while but had been dragging my feet. The second after our meeting ended, I called the Center for Women's Health. Professor MacCurdy told me the guy who raped me is dangerous, referencing the event where he choked my friend for touching me. No one had ever said that to me. It started to shift my mindset from shaming myself and victim blaming to anger and outrage. That is when my writing started gaining more description in the second draft. Per the stages in *The Writing Cure* Chapter 10, I was in Stages 2 and 3. I was telling, not showing in my description of the sexual assault. I wrote "I can't breathe; he's pushing down too hard. I can't breathe through my nose either. Every time I try to breathe in it gets caught." I found it very difficult to communicate my feelings about the event to the audience in a way that wasn't just telling them what happened. I felt safer hiding behind the bland words, because if I used imagery the story would come alive, and God knows what else.

For my third draft of the essay that I finally titled "It was dark," I took all of the important moments from both drafts and combined them into one longer piece. I met with Professor MacCurdy, and I told her that I had so much more to say, so she encouraged me to get it all out. That is exactly what I did. I wrote a list of every triggering memory I could remember that stuck out to me, and I slowly checked them off. Some of them were very detailed while others were vaguer. The vague and unclear ones were the early memories about my family and traumatic situations I stumbled upon or was forced into as a young girl. I was simultaneously in Stage 2 in the scenes with my family and in Stage 5 in the scenes with Adam. I wrote the scenes with my family in the first person but left out important context about who the family members are and how they fit into my life story. In the *Writing Cure*, Stage 5 of the chart is "Individual elaborates and explores own feelings, using an inner referent" (Lutgendorf and Ullrich 181). I was slowly able to write more detail in each draft, because it little by little started coming back to me. In order to communicate my feelings through my words, I was completely showing and not telling. An example in my final draft is the following: "His straight hair is disheveled. He sits slouching and leaning over into my corner [of the couch]. My hands are still shaking. It's darker outside now. It all looks very grey. There is no sun hitting the painting. The only light comes from the silenced movie flickering across the screen. My back is to the screen. I stand so close to it that I can feel its heat." I felt like I was able to put myself in the moment. I was able to feel what I felt then. I could feel the betrayal. He hurt me. I knew that something was wrong, that whatever just happened was wrong. I learned in this class that I had a lot to grieve. The guy who raped me was my friend. Then he was my boyfriend. He said he loved me and then he broke me. I never let myself feel that pain until I started writing at this level.

At the beginning of this class, I felt like my life had sort of skipped by my sexual assault, but I was still stuck there. In chapter eight of *The Writing Cure*, Kitty Klein discusses the link between life stress and working memory capacity and maps out the link in a chart. She says that "memory reconstructions of stressful experiences are fragmented and poorly organized," (142) but this structure makes them highly accessible. Everyone was moving on including the rapist, and I was stuck reliving everything all the time. I had started seeing Adam everywhere, walking to class or in the dining hall, even though he was on a different continent. I would do a double take and realize that the person I saw was too short or not lanky enough. This is also represented in chapter eight. Klein writes, "...the sensory features of stressful experiences are actually represented in a separate knowledge system that is accessed automatically in response to external or internal stimuli that are similar to the experience. When the self-memory system cannot suppress these highly accessible memories, they erupt into consciousness as unwanted and involuntary thoughts" (Klein 143). These traumatic memories never got stored properly in my memory, so whenever there are any external or internal stimuli my body and mind react. Whenever I saw a guy that looked anything like Adam, maybe they had similar hair, glasses, or clothes, my memories would be triggered, and intrusive thoughts of my sexual assault would arise.

For example, one night I was walking back to my dorm room from class. It was completely dark outside. I had been extremely anxious during class, because I saw who I thought was Adam through the window. And what freaked me out even more was that he didn't turn back into who he really was at all. I had also received a call from my counselor, whom I had previously talked with about family trauma that did not involve me, but did weigh heavily on me. It acted as an "external stimuli" as it was similar to my sexual assault (Klein 143). Then in class we talked about the issue of sexual assault for the entire class, the politics, psychology, and intersectionality of it, and everything that was said hit home. The class acted as more "external stimuli." It felt like a punch to my tear ducts. So after class I walked back towards my dorm, and I just felt like a mess. I felt unsafe. My anxiety was skyrocketing, and I felt like curling up in a ball in a corner of a building and crying. I couldn't stop thinking that Adam was everywhere, and I kept looking behind me. I was seconds away from a full-blown panic attack due to all of the "external stimuli." I managed to pull myself out of it when I saw people I knew, for fear of being vulnerable.

Klein states that expressive writing produces improvements in the working memory capacity according to studies through making the "memory structures of [the] stressful experiences more coherent [and] organized" (141). This would explain why after completing the course I had fewer panic attacks and intrusive thoughts about my sexual assault. As we learned in class, writers need to allow themselves to go back to the actual moments of the trauma and describe what they heard and saw. Those memories are still there, intact, and they need to be "described and integrated into the rest of life" as my teacher said, which is what I needed to do. That gets the moments out of us and down on the page, so we can get past them. This is best done with the help of others—friends, family, therapists, teachers, whoever feels safe and appropriate.

The people who helped me during this writing process were Professor MacCurdy, the counselor, and my classmate, Claire. They all became witnesses to my story. Claire was a vital part of my journey. Similar to an example in MacCurdy's *The Mind's Eye,* I worked with Claire who read my essays and was extremely passionate and angered for me, just as Ange was angered for Sarah; as Professor MacCurdy writes in her book: "Ange needed to react honestly, to allow herself to get angry, in order to demonstrate to Sarah another way to respond to this horrific story. The witness provides a safe mirror in which the survivor can see herself and her responses" (136). Ange's anger helped her feel like she had someone on her side, just as Claire did for me. Claire was my witness. Her anger reminded me that this was rape, and it does not magically become okay over time. It's not something that becomes less. She did not diminish my experiences as I felt the passing of time and the people around me did. She didn't blame me or judge me for not being able to move on like time and everyone else around me did. The sexual assault was a traumatic memory that could not be processed into my working memory. I wrote the following on my phone in the car on a particularly rough day early in September of 2021 about my sexual assault: "Society just wants you to move on, move past it. IF I FUCKING COULD I WOULD. It has been almost six years. I should be able to move on. Yet here we are." That line really resonated with Claire when she was editing my essay. And it reminded me that we as survivors did not ask for this. Don't you think if we could just forget about this we would?

When I found out later that she was also a survivor of sexual assault, we talked after class, and I had never felt more heard or more understood in my entire life. I wanted to cry and scream *finally! Someone who gets it.* The importance of community was made apparent to me. Neither she nor I had ever felt so seen, heard, respected, justified, or free. MacCurdy in chapter three of *The Mind's Eye,* discusses the importance of community. She writes, "in their book *Testimony* Shoshana Felman and Dori Laub argue that personal and cultural recovery from trauma requires a conversation between the victim and a witness, that indeed the witness is an utter necessity to complete the cycle of truth-telling," (129). We bore witness to each other with the understanding that we both have felt the sting of isolation.

Society shames sexual assault victims. It makes them into outcasts. Even renowned research psychologists like Christine Blasey Ford, as we discussed in class, was ridiculed for speaking out about her sexual assault that she testified was perpetrated by Supreme Court Justice Brett Kavanaugh. Society teaches you to think that rape was some guy in a white van kidnapping you on the side of the street. We're not taught to watch out for family members or friends. I was not taught to watch out for boys who told you they loved you. People want to believe that rape is some fluke accident. They want to blame the victim, because they don't want to live in a world where they have no control. Sadly, it happens more than people would like to think.

I also felt this fear of being out of control in an uncontrollable situation after I was raped. I was grasping for control and was blaming myself to avoid the fact that I truly had no control. The innate human fear of being out of control is terrifying for everyone. No one wants to acknowledge that they really have no power. I never wanted to feel that weak and vulnerable again, so I controlled what I could. I became a perfectionist. I got perfect grades. I had a set, concrete plan for the future. I limited what I ate to only "healthy" foods, and if there were none I didn't eat. I looked a certain way. I acted a certain way. I was nice and pleasant, but stern and cold, so no one would hurt me like that again. I thought that if I put on the hard shell of a bitch maybe I would be safe. I would never let anyone take advantage of me, but at the same time accepted "love" from people in my family and other partners who treated me terribly because it was fundamentally ingrained in me, from my childhood and my assault, that some abuse is okay.

During this process of writing, I became beside myself with anger at my parents and my family in general. I blamed them for my sexual assault. My justification was that they did not teach me about consent or sex. They knew what happened with Adam. They should've put me in therapy even if I didn't want to go as my school guidance counselor told them to. They should've been on me, watching for warning signs of depression, anxiety, suicidal thoughts, and PTSD. I was fourteen, nowhere near an adult, and nowhere near being able to handle this alone. But that's what I did. I blamed the school too, for skipping my grade's sex education. For relying on the parents of our entire grade to teach us about sex that they neglected to teach. It was serious negligence on the school's part.

During this process, I gained some significant insights into my trauma. For example, Professor MacCurdy asked me once why Adam was so scary. It brought up a memory I had suppressed a long time ago. The first time I hung out with Adam, we watched the movie, Kill Bill, with another friend of mine. This was one of his favorite movies of all time. He worshiped Quentin Tarantino. The opening scene of Kill Bill is Uma Thurman being raped while unconscious in a hospital bed. The movie was almost foreshadowing what happened to me. It showed me his perception of women and sex.

Another insight I gained from this process of writing is the ability to see Adam as a perpetrator. Professor MacCurdy said to me, "It could have been anyone; it just happened to be you." That was one of the most freeing things I have ever heard. It helped open my eyes. Then the act of mapping out all of the events before and after the rape allowed me to open my eyes completely. I stopped listening to Adam's voice, and I heard the fourteen-year-old girl's voice for once in my life. I had secretly blamed myself for the rape for a long time. I was always thinking *he didn't force me, he didn't tie me down, I wasn't unconscious, so why didn't I fight back.* I always thought that there was something I could do to avoid this. I should've seen it coming. But because of mapping my trauma down I saw his manipulation of me. I saw the fear that he instilled in my fourteen-year-old self. I knew he was violent, and I knew he had a temper. All of my suspicions were confirmed at a friend's birthday party. Adam choked a guy for touching and flirting with me. He ran up to us, grabbed Will, and knocked me to the ground. In the final draft of "It Was Dark," I wrote "he keeps his arm bent across Will's neck. Will sputters, grasping at Adam's arm, his face turning beet red, tears gleaming in his eyes. I don't even know what I see in Adam's eyes." Because of this traumatic event I can see how truly terrifying Adam was/is. During the evening of the sexual assault, I knew his patience was wearing thin and that he would hurt me if I kept saying no.

There were some negative side effects of this psychological process. Because it was only a thirteen-week class, we had to expedite this process. In Chapter three of *Opening Up: The Healing Power of Expressing Emotion*, James Pennebaker and Sandra Beall discuss a study where they had groups of college students either write about superficial topics or traumatic experiences in one of three different perspectives: venting their emotions, facts of their trauma, or both. They soon found out that "writing about horrible things made people feel horrible immediately after writing," (Pennebaker 34). This is what I experienced after beginning to write about my trauma. I felt horrible every time I sat down to write and after. I did not feel the "emotional release that should result in feelings of relief and contentment" that Sandra believes is the catharsis after venting one's emotions (Pennebaker 34). Pennebaker also noted that "many [students] reported dreaming or continually thinking about their writing topics over the four days of the study," (32). Like the students in the study, I also was dreaming and continually thinking about my sexual assault. I had a two-week period of time where I was extremely stressed and anxious. I was seeing Adam everywhere. I almost left college to go home. I was calling my boyfriend every day in tears. I was dissociating during conversations with my friends. I was having nightmares every night. I had one about being sexually assaulted by a family member and one about a guy raping me in my dorm room bed. I had to miss class because of panic attacks. I emailed my teachers and skipped some schoolwork. I lived the effects that Pennebaker and Beall observed in their study.

Their study continued to go on for 5 ½ months after the experiment. It showed that the students who wrote about their deepest thoughts and feelings surrounding trauma had "improved moods, more positive outlook and greater physical health [(i.e. fewer illness visits to the health center)]" (Pennebaker 34). In this thirteen-week class we did not have the luxury to see how this psychological process of writing about your trauma affects us in the long term. At the end of the semester, I left with a strong feeling of uncertainty. I didn't know if there would ever be a moment where my writing would feel complete, and I would feel healed. I didn't know if I would ever reach Stage 7 of *The Writing Cure*, Stage 7 being when the "individual had an emerging understanding and integration of past issues in a new way; these have meaning for other areas in a person's life" (Lutgendorf and Ullrich 181). But I did finish the course with a new network of people dedicated to my health and well-being. I immediately went into eating disorder recovery. I got my vitals checked biweekly and a nutritionist to help me build a meal plan. I attended weekly therapy sessions and got on anxiety medication.

I can proudly say that now I have reached Stage 7, less than three years later. My panic attacks have gone down to almost nonexistent. My PTSD symptoms have lessened, and my overall anxiety levels have dropped significantly. I'm well into my eating disorder recovery; I love food again. I have no symptoms of depression or suicidal thoughts. I have an increased love for life and my quality of life has increased dramatically. This occurred with the assistance of my amazing therapist and doctors and my unrelenting love for myself.

I also made the incredibly brave decision to file a police report. Like many other survivors, my greatest fear was going to court and being defamed, shamed, or called a liar. This was one of the most life-changing decisions. On recommendation from the police officer on my case, I filed and received an emergency 10-day restraining order. Then at the 10-Day Hearing, I faced Adam and his lawyer. It was terrifying and intimidating. I waited a grueling two hours in court, with Adam smiling at me and trying to continually make eye contact with me and my family. I chased off panic attack after panic attack. Then I stood in front of a judge. I had a victim advocate standing with me, but she wasn't allowed to speak for me. And I had my parents, my partner of five years, and his mother, and the detective on my case behind me supporting me in court. I had to advocate for myself to the judge, to Adam's lawyer. After a lengthy hearing, I was granted a year-long restraining order. I honestly couldn't believe it. When the judge said it, I turned behind me in shock to see my partner's warm, encouraging smile and my mom with tears in her eyes. They all know the hell I had gone through. And here I was fighting back and breaking my silence. And I won. I left the courtroom surrounded by my family, crying with relief. I felt the energy shift in me. A million tons had been released from my body. I felt lighter than I had in years.

For years I had been experiencing severe menstrual cramps, and they had been ramping up over the two years. A couple weeks prior to the court hearing, I was diagnosed with severe dysmenorrhea. I was told there was nothing I could do except add more hormonal birth control (which I did not want to do) or take a high dosage of Ibuprofen three times a day, which would hurt my digestive tract (I already had IBS). The cramps were waking me up at night and it was an uncontrollable amount of pain where I would scream and cry. I was incapacitated on my period for days every month. It was prohibiting me from working, studying, and going out. It was concerning for everyone around me. It just wasn't normal. The next day after the court hearing, I got my period, and my menstrual pain was cut down to half. The only change was the court hearing. And I knew it was the best decision I had ever made. It reaffirmed to me how necessary this was for me and my healing journey.

During this course, I stopped running. I started talking and claimed my narrative. I started listening to the only important voice— mine. I shined a light on anything scary. I face my fears, and I have continued to live that mantra every day since. Although this process has not been easy, this class helped me get the professional help I've needed for five years. That one cannot put a price on. Narrative medicine saved my life.

After this class, my life was not magically easier, but I was in a better place to face the ups and downs. I stopped fighting the past every day and was able to focus my energy on now. Since the class, I studied abroad at Oxford University and interned at the UMass Press. I lost my childhood best friend to suicide in Fall of 2023 during my final semester of undergrad. This hit me so hard in a way where I, an honors A+ student, nearly didn't graduate. With the help of my professors, and my partner, I was able to graduate as planned, a semester early in December of 2023, and walked in the May graduation with my friends.

My journey is far from over. And I know there are many obstacles to come. But I am willing to dive into the uncertain unknowns again and again, for myself and for the little girl in me. Because if I learned anything from this, I learned that I'm a survivor and I deserve to thrive. And I can thrive.

Reflections from Marian

Sarah began the class in the wake of a terrifying experience that she could not initially recognize as sending her into post-traumatic stress disorder. The problems here are two-fold: first she was preyed upon by someone she thought was her friend; second, the assault was complicated by a surrounding rape culture that normalizes predatory behaviors and makes it difficult for victims to recognize what has happened to them. Our culture is replete with images of sexual predation made to appear common, perhaps even expected, and certainly overwhelming.

The trauma in these situations is two-fold: first, such sexualized overpowering can create victims that lose their sense of personal autonomy and power and often feel shame for being victimized. They can lose the ability to see themselves as capable of self-protection from harm. Second, they can take that shame on themselves and become isolated in a world that takes such sexualized behaviors for granted and does not acknowledge the harm they do, especially to the young. This means they can see themselves as victims who cannot protect themselves and who don't even know if they are supposed to protect themselves. If this sexualized behavior is taken for granted, is there something wrong with them that they find it scary, even traumatic? Such attacks can make those on the receiving end feel victimized: how can they learn to protect themselves if they were so "easily" overwhelmed already?

Often the first response to being a victim of such a crime can be —put it away. Move on. Forget about it. As Sarah said in her essay, "I felt like it was over and in the past." Writers must decide themselves if they want to address such moments and if they do, when. I let Sarah know that if she wanted to write about what happened, I would read it, but that this was her decision. It is essential to let writers decide their topics themselves as well as if they want to share their work since trauma can already make survivors feel out of control. Yet sharing these experiences with others can provide allies that can help to confront the effect of the perpetrator. It is hard to do this alone—and why would we want to? One of the worst parts of trauma is the isolation it causes. If we confront that first by creating a bridge to another person, we at least know we have an ally, and the first consequence of trauma—isolation--is addressed.

When Sarah told me her perpetrator attacked a friend, the sole thought I had was this guy is dangerous. She needed to call the authorities, but she had to come to this decision herself. Anything else could only make her feel more out of control. But once she realized how others saw her attacker, that her response was utterly rational, she could act, knowing this would protect others as well as herself: "I started to shift my mindset from shaming myself and victim blaming to anger and outrage." Interestingly, only after that could she begin to write a clear description of this attack. Shame is a frequent result of trauma survival since victims often blame themselves. But once survivors recognize that the perpetrator is the only culprit, they can step outside the shame and tell the truth. Once Sarah gave herself permission to tell the story she was able to write the descriptive details that were driving her emotional memories: "I never let myself feel the pain until I started writing at this level." Being heard, being seen, is perhaps the most important part of this process. Shame and fear often silence survivors, but telling their stories can break through that wall and allow them to connect with others. This can be the most helpful moment of all: "Finally! Someone who gets it!" as Sarah wrote.

Sarah's experience with sexual abuse is, most unfortunately, not rare. In my teaching experience over the years many of my female students—and a few of the males— have written about such experiences. In his excellent book, *Empathic Teaching*, Jeffrey Berman argues, "It may be far riskier not to allow our students to write about their fear and conflicts" (375). He suggests that students write about what they are most afraid of because when they do, they survive the very terrors that threaten to silence them. While I can understand the impulse to suggest this assignment, I leave it open. I tell my students that I will read whatever they write, since I find that when writers come to their topics freely and on their own, this leads to a deeper ownership of their writing which can produce a safer process and perhaps a better outcome.

As Sarah wrote, this process takes time, and it is essential for writers to have a support system to go to if needed. Sarah wrote about the new network of people she put in her life to assist her: doctors, therapists, nutritionists, all chosen by her to facilitate her growth. But most important she learned that she is a survivor who has learned to thrive in the face of life's challenges. The class readings also helped her to theorize and contextualize her experience to help her make sense of these events and her response to them. Equally important are the connections built in the class that allow writers to find community among those with whom they share their stories.

Sarah's remarkable journey and moving essay remind us that a primary purpose of education is to give our students the tools they need to create their own best lives, free of coercion and fear, and then if, in spite of our best efforts, trauma crashes into their lives, to give them the tools to save themselves from its worst effects and to achieve agency by learning how to tell our stories so they don't tell us. This kind of education is not only an asset: it is a necessity.

Works Cited

ABC News—See hppts://abcnews.go.com Dec. 7, 2023

Barry, Ellen, "Brain Study Suggests Traumatic Memories Are Processed as Present Experience," *NYT,* November 30, 2023.

Berman, Jeffrey. *Empathic Teaching: Education for Life*. Amherst: University of Massachusetts Press, 2004.

Clifton, Lucille. Keynote Address. Conference of the Association for Poetry Therapy, Columbia, Md, May 6, 1996.

Gere, Anne Ruggles. "Whose Voice Is It Anyway?" In *Writing and Healing: Toward an Informed Practice*. National Council of Teachers of English Press, 2000, pp. 25-33.

Ishiguro, Kazio. 2023 AARP Awards Ceremony.

Klein, Kitty. "Stress Expressive Writing and Working Memory." In *The Writing Cure: How Expressive Writing Promotes Health and Emotional Well-Being*. Washington: American Psychological Association, 2002, pp. 135-56.

Lanius, Ruth, *NYT,* November 30, 2023.

Lepore, Stephen J. and Joshua Smyth. *The Writing Cure: How Expressive Writing Promotes Health and Emotional Well-Being*. American Psychological Association, 2002.

Lutgendorf, Susan K. and Philip Ullrich ."Cognitive Processing, Disclosure, and Health: Psychological and Physiological Mechanisms." In *The Writing Cure: How Expressive Writing Promotes Health and Emotional Well-Being*. Washington, American Psychological Association, 2002, pp. 177-96.

MacCurdy, Marian. *The Mind's Eye: Image and Memory in Writing About Trauma*. Amherst, MA: University of Massachusetts Press, 2007.

Pennebaker, James. *Opening Up:* The Healing Power of Expressing Emotion. New New York: Guilford Press, 1997.

Schiller, Daniela, "Brain Study Suggests Traumatic Memories Are Processed as Present Experience," *NYT,* November 30, 2023.

Van der Kolk, Bessel, Alexander McFarlane, Lars Weisaeth, *Traumatic Stress*, New York: Guilford Press, 1996.

ESSAYS

Mindful Administration: Toward a Theory of Academic Leadership We Can Live With

Sue Doe and Janelle Adsit

This article names barriers to faculty leadership and identifies specific ways that faculty can harness tools and resources needed to lead well. Through mindful and relational leadership practices, faculty can ensure that the values that academic communities espouse are made manifest.

This has been a difficult and vulnerable article to write. It has been an exercise in working through cognitive dissonance and identity-crisis as we navigated leadership roles in two public universities in California and Colorado. Janelle has served as department chair; Sue has been writing program administrator, faculty senate chair, and director of a center for teaching and learning.[1] We

---

1. Janelle became department co-chair in January 2021, in the midst of a crisis point at her university that was contextualized by the pandemic and ongoing budgetary constraints. Janelle stepped into the role mid-way through the academic year when her tenure file was under review. Janelle, with a co-chair (whose tenure file was also under review at the same time), stepped into the role in a time of confusion and instability. In this period, the university administration was "reorganizing" departments in the College, combining academic units to reduce costs. Chairing a department was not in Janelle's career plan, and she felt inadequately prepared to lead.

Sue came to administrative work as an outgrowth of her participation in a rhetoric and composition program in which the faculty do rotations into and out of various writing program administration roles, or where at least that has been the long-held goal. Sue had experience with both writing center and writing-across-the-curriculum administration as well as with leading a campus writing integration initiative. She eventually took a rotation as writing program administrator, directing first-year and advanced composition and managing eight core curriculum writing courses. She held this role for five years although the standard was three, and then she was elected to be Chair of the Faculty Council (Senate) which involved liaising with upper administration in addition to leading shared governance processes for the faculty as a whole. Elected for each of three one-year terms in beginning at the start of the pandemic in March of 2020, she was soon thrust into high-level discussions around an athletics scandal, around an absence of diversity and social justice orientations in the curriculum, and in a complete university restructure of the administration involving the termination of the President. At the end of this term-limited role, Sue then applied for and was selected to administer the university's teaching and learning center, leaving the English Department where there seemed nowhere to go except back into the administration of the writing program. She maintains her tenure line

have been outwardly successful in these roles, but inwardly dissatisfied with not only the effectiveness of our efforts but the toll on our persons.

Upon entering our positions, we quickly recognized that we were lacking a theory of leadership to guide our decisions and practices. We stepped into midlevel faculty leadership roles without a clear framework or compass to orient our actions. While our classroom practice has been supported by a pedagogical philosophy informed by scholarship that weighs the politics and potential of our choices in working with students, our leadership practice had no equivalent. We had no articulated leadership praxis to help us navigate the moment-to-moment complexity of institutional life. This absence became a pressing concern as we faced increasingly high-stakes decisions and ethical challenges in our administrative work.

In response, we turned to self-study as a method of inquiry. We endeavored not only to understand what we were doing, but why. We made many attempts to reflect on the exigencies we felt but could often not name: we kept hour-by-hour work-logs, identifying our in-the-moment decision-making and naming where our time and energies were spent; we kept track of anecdotes as snapshots of ourselves doing the messy work of navigating life within these roles. While we ultimately left these methods behind, we continued to write this article over the span of five years. These years were shaped by significant cultural and political upheaval, defined in the context of the Black Lives Matter movement, the global pandemic, and the first Trump administration. We write in a context of threats not only to public education but to the very idea of intellectual freedom. We feel acutely the stakes of our work—and the necessity of courageous, steadfast, and responsive leadership—in this political moment.

In the years of writing this we met as co-authors regularly, often on a weekly basis, to reflect on our experiences. The conversations became a way for us each to process what was occurring in our immediate circumstances. Slowly—with many interruptions and through frustration and overwhelm—we came to name our situation: The administrative aspects of faculty life often feel soul-sucking, but abandoning them entirely is not an option; there is too much at stake.

More than just a set of coping mechanisms or managerial tactics, what we needed was a robust theory and model—one capable of holding the complexity of leadership and acknowledging the "betwixt and between" nature of our roles. Our work exists in an interstitial space: between policy and pedagogy, between bureaucracy and imagination, between the institutional and the personal. It became clear to us that claiming space for a thoughtful reconceptualization of leadership—one deeply informed by the theoretical and academic work

---

today, but less of her role looks like a faculty one although she constantly finds herself explaining faculty perspectives to administrators and staff.

we engage in as scholars—was both urgent and necessary. We are interested in moving into this under-theorized terrain deliberately, claiming and naming it as legitimate intellectual and institutional work. Leadership, we argue, should not exist outside or beneath the scholarly disciplines, but rather as an integral part of them. It is a conversation that belongs squarely in the realm of theory and praxis, and one that must be treated with the same critical rigor and reflective seriousness that we bring to our teaching and research.

Our goal has been to reclaim agency and to hold tight to our values in the tumult of the administrative role. Our administrative lives are not ancillary to our academic missions; they are central to the ongoing project of making universities livable, ethical, and intellectually honest spaces.

Our effort is not to absolve or romanticize administration, nor to pathologize it, but to examine how roles are constructed. Rhetorics that stigmatize administration as the "red pill" or the "dark side" often carry with them a pernicious purism; a refusal to engage with the "dirty work" of institutional maintenance also maintains the hierarchies of the status quo. To dismiss administrative work on these terms often functions as a kind of denial, an abdication of responsibility at a time when leadership is desperately needed.

What We Mean by 'Task Mind'

Through our methods of self-examination, we found that we were regularly enacting what we came to refer to as "task mind" —a shorthand term that we use to describe the reactive, agitated state of "putting out fires" and "task-mastering" our way through the roles we have taken on.

While we don't wish to generalize—i.e., not all administrative life is characterized by this mindset, nor is the phenomenon we describe limited to administration— this reactive, hyper-vigilant state may be prompted and perpetuated by institutional conditions. The term "task mind" is imperfect as a description of the default approach to administrative work that we found in ourselves. The term's simplicity risks erasing the hierarchies and privileges that shape who gets to perform which forms of labor, and how that labor is valued. Ultimately, we chose to stay with the term not because it resolves these tensions, but because it keeps them visible. Writing together has made us aware of how language itself can reproduce the very elitism we seek to critique, and our considerations in naming became a mirror for our own assumptions about intellectual labor, effort, and worth.

Our act of naming was ultimately an attempt to become better observers of ourselves. As we've experienced it, task mind is a "haze" generated as the sympathetic nervous system pushes through the basic stresses of a given day, enacting forms of work far less onerous than the labor carried out by the majority of workers on this planet. With little recognition of our own relative power and capability to interrupt the "business-as-usual," we keep moving with the inertia of task mind. The signs of our obedience to it are in our bodies: the physical dis-ease of the Zoom calls we stay seated for, the Pavlovian addiction to the sound-signature of an arriving email, the nightly bouts of insomnia and associated panic about issues that are not worthy of the strain on our hearts and metabolisms—especially when measured against the profound and consequential harms endured in the world beyond our screens.

The physical cost of such labor is felt differently by different bodies, as it is also exacerbated by racism, heteronormativity and homophobia, cis-sexism, ableism, and other forms of intersectional oppression. We write with this embodied reality as our exigence, as we also attend to the implications of our actions: of the complicity that comes from handling the next thing in front of us with little regard for how a given decision contributes to broader goals. Task mind is a kind of self-coercion and delusion that is ultimately "mindless," as a form of "monkey mind." Christy L. Wenger offers these terms in *Yoga Minds, Writing Bodies*, to describe the tendency toward "unthinkingly reacting to everything that comes our way." Whereas mindfulness is a "practice of reconnecting with ourselves… to give measure to our actions, teaching us that we can control our response to stimuli by listening to our bodies and using our energy productively" (ix). Task mind is, in contrast, an anxious unawareness, and it may bring about a range of unfavorable experiences—even some that may border on the comic or the absurd, such as it did for us in Fall 2022:

> At the end of a typically stressful week in her role as chair, Janelle found herself literally lost in a 1,200 acre forest in the middle of the night, walking with her department's program leader. Out for what they thought would be a quick "walk and debrief" of the afternoon's department meeting they had facilitated, the two became so immersed in their conversation about department processes that they lost track of space and time, with very limited cell phone service and no food or water. They disrupted a colleague's evening with a text message with their GPS location, asking to be found.[1] When the county sheriff rescued them at midnight, seven hours and many miles from where they had started, the conversation about work still continued in the back of the police car. The experience of work culture was so consuming that it can literally make one lose one's way.
>
> In the Fall of 2022, near the start of her final year as the chair of the faculty senate, Sue fell while out for a run and injured her dominant hand.

---

1. Thanks to Renée Byrd for most kind help in this moment of need.

The partially detached tendons might have healed if she had rested her hand, but instead she resumed work from her laptop almost immediately, altering the use of her fingers on the keyboard. A few months later, due to overuse, she had detached the tendons completely and now was thrust into physical and occupational therapy to prepare the hand for surgery. Nine months after the original injury, she had surgery, but this was just two weeks after starting a new administrative position directing the teaching and learning center so she did not feel she could take time off or depend for long on voice-to-text software to do her keyboarding for her. She returned to work too quickly, and another nine months later needed a re-do of the surgery with the doctor saying, "I detect a pattern here. You're going to have to assure me that you will rest your hand for six to eight weeks before we move forward with a second surgery." The injury to her dominant hand was bad enough; more concerning still was a work ethic so ingrained that care of the self was out of the question. Sue's good fortune in having been healthy most of her life now showed itself for what it was— an internalized ableism and a substantial conceit, a self-effacement and stoicism that was not only a misplaced source of pride but an obstacle to healing.

We are cognizant of the privilege of being able to preoccupy ourselves with work culture, the privilege of being able to trust in our survival and to be able to call for help. The privilege of unlimited trips to occupational therapy and insurance coverage for not one but two surgeries—the privilege even of writing about all of this during work hours. Our privilege as tenured white women in the academy also allows for the work behaviors we've fallen into; work can be at the forefront of our minds only because our basic needs are met. We share our experience not because it is generalizable but because it perhaps can provide a lens on the university apparatus that conditions us and that we have in many ways given ourselves over to. We are complicit in its workings. To find a form of faculty leadership[2] we can live with—a form of leadership that supports our own and others' living—is about more than helping ourselves and others with an immediate problem of distraction, overwhelm, and burnout; it is about the broader objectives of higher education and the ethos of leadership that our educational values require.

---

2. We define faculty leaders as those who either choose or are thrust into leadership of programs, centers, departments or governance committees and who possess the training associated with faculty roles and criteria for selection. For the purposes of our discussion, we distinguish faculty leadership from that of vice presidents, vice provosts, and deans who may have "retreat rights" to a faculty position but were not hired into a faculty research or teaching role.

Some of the Broader Problems of Academic Leadership

As we sought a theory of faculty leadership we could live with—one that is aligned with our values and that would complement our orientations as teachers and scholars—we first looked close to home, writing studies scholarship, which has a long history of theorizing faculty leadership in the role of the Writing Program Administrator, or WPA, due in part, to the fact that writing programs are vexed by many of the same leadership challenges as universities generally. WPAs manage large programs that involve significant investment in faculty who have opportunity (and obligation) to address the needs of nearly all undergraduates who are variously prepared for college. WPAs participate in capitalist labor practices that bring together a small number of tenure-line "bosses" (Sledd), "droids" (Nelson), "faculty-managers" (Klausman); and "lower-level management in the managed university" (Bousquet 496) with a large number of contingent faculty who generally possess little job security. WPAs and their programs have generally had to shift, or be conciliatory, to meet the needs of not only students but the current priorities of their institutions (Skinnell). Yet while theories of WPA praxis have become increasingly robust, including the feminist orientations articulated by Casie Fedukovich and Sue Doe as well as Laura Micciche and Donna Strickland, it is also the case, as Strickland points out, that WPAs often undergo a tacit, undertheorized, and "unofficial schooling in the management of…teachers and programs" (1)—an "unofficial schooling" that most often happens on the job. Such schooling is generally inadequate to the task of providing the leadership praxis that writing programs most need, much less leadership at higher levels of university administration.

More specifically, faculty who find themselves leading programs or departments may rarely have cause or opportunity to consider the values that guide day-to-day decision-making, to convey vision, objectives, and ethical codes to self and others, or to find touchpoints/supports to encourage deliberate reflection within a community of practice of fellow leaders. For example, faculty leaders rarely take part in a dedicated and sustained mentoring program. They/we may be exposed to "chair training" or required to complete an HR-mandated training for supervisors, but such efforts are mired in administrative compliance—not vision and strategy. The absence of the genres and forums that would facilitate a reflective orientation to leadership is symptomatic of our circumstances: we become utterly consumed by all the work it takes to make the machine operate and are thus distracted from thoughtfully applying our theoretical frames as leaders. As a result, we too often don't contemplate, much less articulate, the rationale behind what we are doing, and in the process become all the more susceptible to the trends of disaffection with leadership itself. Similarly, faculty who become leaders within governance units such as faculty senates are often inadequately prepared as well, a problem that Robert Scott, in the *Journal of Academic Freedom* described this way: "Unfortunately, few campuses devote resources to preparing faculty members for their roles and responsibilities for governance or for leadership in faculty committees and senates. As a consequence, faculty are sometimes criticized for not fulfilling their governing roles adequately. But the fault lies with trustees and presidents who pay too little attention to this important dimension of university governance and leadership" (4).

When faculty do become leaders at higher levels of their universities, the implications of their shortcomings compound and complicate. The individualist nature of faculty life with respect to its expectations and rewards can too often become a failure to do broad systems thinking, as institutional conventions tend to treat faculty members as if each were an independent entrepreneur instead of a small component of a larger whole. Under such circumstances, even well-intended decision-making may proceed without sufficient thinking about downstream effects (Lane). Structures that work well for faculty in traditional research and teaching roles may be wildly out of step with current trends and university formations. For instance, if today's faculty have elected out of, or been shielded from, conversations about competency-based learning and short-term certificate and micro-credential programs, they may be unaware of how poorly the traditional semester aligns with current thinking about postsecondary access, new-learner populations, and work-learn cycles (Zalaznick). A significant additional danger in leaving faculty out of such conversations is that they (we) then do not offer critical feedback as decisions move forward.

We note that the challenges associated with cultivating leaders are not limited to the higher education setting, nor is the desire "not to lead" an attribute strictly belonging to faculty. In 2006, Thomas Tierney predicted a "leadership deficit" due to a failure of organizations to cultivate new leaders; organizations instead allow individuals to "fall into" leadership or be pressed into service rather than to aspire to the challenges of leading. The international nonprofit APQC (American Productivity and Quality Center), which provides training and consultation to over 1000 organizations and 45 industries worldwide, reports that this leadership deficit derives from an absence of attention to developing among employees the major competencies associated with effective leadership—strategic thinking, change management, knowledge sharing, listening, and emotional intelligence—with the result being dependence on leaders who are mired in traditional ways of thinking (Lam). Similarly, Frances Kunreuther and Sean Thomas-Breitfeld, writing for *The Chronicle of Philanthropy* in 2024, reported that persons of color were moving into leadership roles at nonprofit organizations more to correct deficits in leadership representation than to support the active cultivation of their leadership potential. In 2023, the Neuroleadership Institute pointed to post-pandemic causes for the current unmet need for new leaders, including the several years of lockdown that reduced the pipeline of leaders, remote work practices that led to reduced visibility of emerging leaders, and the articulation of new priorities among workers themselves. Nick Lynch, writing for *Forbes* in 2024, called out many of the same trends and factors and recommended a shift in organizational culture focusing on less rigid work requirements and efforts to "foster a culture of abundance and collaboration" in which there's focus on "building strong relationships and trust." Together these many indicators suggest that many sectors are grappling with ways to be mindful of the humanity of potential leaders. Perhaps we are at a time when leadership itself is being called to change in order to reflect pandemic-era realizations, such as the reasonableness and effectiveness of flexible work arrangements, the importance of cultures that celebrate the wholeness of people, the value of genuinely collaborative approaches, and the insistence on self-preservation. In this context, university administrators are reporting burnout, yet often, due to their positions, feel unable to say so. Unable to express their suffering or take time for self-care, they have been leaving administrative work in droves. A 2021 report shows that search firms were experiencing unprecedented low levels of interest in administrative positions, even at chair and dean levels (Perlmutter).

Perhaps part of the problem is that governing boards of universities and the faculty, alongside even those who come up through the faculty to become administrators, have differing views of leadership, even in terms of their university president. It has been said that "boards look increasingly to the president as a corporate-style leader, [while] faculty members still expect a president to be the academic-in-chief" (Kelderman). And faculty often feel that the corporate processes that universities have embraced since at least the 1980s—see George Keller's *Academic Strategy: The Management Revolution in Higher Education*—work at cross purposes to faculty values, imposing "uninspiring linearity of goal, objective, and action" as well as "the mechanistic progression from environmental scan, value proposition, mission, vision, strategic matrix, key performance indicators, and implementation benchmarks and milestones" (Utz). Perhaps most tellingly the language of corporatized university leadership has trended toward words like "agility" and "nimbleness"—terms that are associated with war, sports, and dog training. As Richard Utz points out, the term "agility" derives directly from the Westminster Kennel Club's description of a [dog] breed's standard of performance in relation to its owner-handler.

For some very good reasons, then, faculty may resist "the call to lead," perhaps in part because we fear what we might become or what we are becoming part of. Stepping into leadership may mean stepping away from the traditional rewards and recognitions of faculty; we sense we are giving up that which we were trained and love to do—our scholarship and our teaching. We find it difficult to keep up with the literature in our area, harder still to generate it ourselves. Plus, asked to make tough decisions as administrators, we risk alienating our faculty colleagues. And this is all geometrically much harder for faculty-administrators of color who find themselves shouldering heavier loads while dealing with, for example, "the persistent exhaustion and terror of being Black in the academy" (Simula).

Yet faculty can become effective leaders and change agents, as Emily M. Janke has pointed out, defining the rise of scholar-administrators who "leverage the skill sets, perspectives, networks, and resources they possess—as scholars who continue scholarly approaches and agendas—in their administrative positions to push proactively for change" (110). As Janke points out, many faculty get into administration and leadership due to a desire to see change and because leadership "affords them access to resources and networks that are necessary for change, and which may not be otherwise possible, for example, as a faculty member within an academic department" (110). Similarly, Aaron Coe and Ravi Chinta found in their case study of five scholar-administrators that "the scholar-administrator was more connected to the people within and outside the university, their own field of practice, and with the university than were administrative peers who did not engage in scholarship" (abstract). These scholar-administrators were helping their organizations stay abreast of emerging trends. All in all, it seems there is something to be said of combining a scholarly agenda with leadership and administration, assuming that a reasonable workload distribution can be achieved.

Leadership and Maintenance of the Status Quo

Attention to leadership, as a praxis that is responsive to the ongoing and emergent situations of the academy, is still lacking in our scholarly conversations. Because we don't have a reflective practice that is scaffolded by the field, faculty may fall back on "business as usual" modes when we step into leadership roles. Every action that a faculty member undertakes is going to be part of—and one could argue complicit with—the status quo because it is virtually impossible to work within a system without reinforcing it. Even as the idea of the "campus radical" persists, this figure is, in Vijay Prashad's words, "the domesticated rabble rouser who provides the academy with its illusion of ideological diversity." Yet their potential to radically shift the status quo remains limited. Broadly speaking, faculty leaders may find themselves ill-equipped to use their roles for institutional transformation, succumbing to forces that reward obedience to university norms.[3] As Sara Ahmed observes, "A system is reproduced by rewarding those who are willing to reproduce the system" (100). The pressure to "serve" within

---

3. See also Boggs, Abigail, Eli Meyerhoff, Nick Mitchell, and Zach Schwartz-Weinstein. "Abolitionist University Studies: An Invitation." 2019. Web. https://abolition.university/

the institution may easily slip into being of service to the institution, if one does not have the time, energy, and support to maintain a reflective practice through one's work. There are many forces that reward obedience; this is as true in the classroom as it is in the meeting room: the obedience of the student who obeys the strictures of an assignment runs parallel to the obedience of the faculty member who "plays their part" to the satisfaction of those of higher rank. Those of us with the privilege to have been deemed "good students" within the system are beneficiaries of that system. We in turn find the capital to continue our work in the academy; in such ways are we then poised to replicate its systems and obey its norms, even with the overlay of the criticality and politics we may espouse. Ironically, faculty's embeddedness in extant systems exists alongside the persistent image of faculty as obstinate and obstructionist. Such characterizations may function as administrative justification for why faculty voices are circumscribed. The casting of faculty as withholding and self-serving may be emblematic of the ongoing antagonism between classes that often find themselves pitted against each other on key issues.

> In the midst of strident calls for increased compensation for all employee groups given extreme inflationary pressures, university administration at Sue's institution agreed to a significant across-the-board pay increase but publicly associated those raises with increased tuition (Lyell), thereby deflecting student unhappiness with rising tuition back onto faculty and staff "selfishness." Faculty and staff, not wishing to embitter students, parents, or taxpayers quietly submitted to low or no pay raises for the next few years in order to not appear self-serving, despite the fact that cost-of-living and compensation analyses suggested that pay increases were appropriate and overdue. Faculty and (especially) staff colleagues paid a significant price for faculty unwillingness to step out boldly and challenge the status quo. As the employees with the most job security, it is up to the faculty to show leadership on matters that affect not only themselves but others. Yet faculty are too often reluctant to rock the boat.

At the same time, the system continues to reward those who are perceived as cooperative: faculty who align themselves with administrative priorities may be more likely to receive institutional support—such as a provost's signature on a sabbatical request or a favorable outcome in the tenure process. As Nicholas de Genova writes, "it is the tenure process that serves as the most decisive disciplinary technology within academia" (321). Through such disciplinary mechanisms, faculty are entrusted to maintain institutional values.

---

invitation/ The authors argue against depoliticizing histories and theories of the university that sustain obedience to its status quo.

As chair of faculty senate, Sue places two motions on the senate agenda, one dealing with graduate activity fees that the trustees have agreed to cover, the other dealing with a section of the faculty manual relating to intellectual property and overseen by a broad-based governance group that includes university lawyers. Both agenda items are called back by the president's office due to the anticipated effect of these progressive commitments being codified into the legally binding manual. Simultaneously, a new chief operating officer contacts the chair of the faculty senate to say that he has been charged by university counsel to create a policy committee on policies (to generate a policy on policies!) This policy committee had been created to police the "renegade" faculty whose long service as the writers of policy was no longer needed ... or wanted. The policy experts signal that they intended to manage policy and 'free' the faculty to do their real work: teaching and research, not governance.

Faculty Leadership Roles Are Fraught

With limited resources and ever-increasing demands under the university's "efficiency models," it may be nearly irresistible for faculty to accept an offer to focus on just one of the so-called "pillars" of the professoriate: to just "teach" or just "do research." However, this phenomenon results in a class stratification of the university that serves to consolidate decision-making power, along with the benefits of institutional wealth, in the hands of the few—i.e., those who hold full-time administrative positions and are themselves managed by governing boards that are authorized by state governments and philanthropic shareholding. The aspects of faculty life (i.e., research, teaching, service) continue to be divided and compartmentalized within the Taylorism of university corporate policy (Brown; Kezar and Sam).[4] And stewarding the university, which is to say leading, appears nowhere in this stratified efficiency model of faculty labor but is instead relinquished to the administrative class—with an associated forfeiture of participative governance and aspirations toward an inclusive intellectual community. Faculty leadership is curtailed and granted limited access to decision-making power, sometimes without even a seat at the table of actual governance. Faculty leader-

---

4. The most obvious casualties of the debundled faculty are the contingent teaching faculty, who, off the tenure track and generally responsible for little new knowledge production, carry hypnotically high teaching loads that in turn maintains a class division that maintains their colleagues, the tenurable research faculty at levels above them in this constructed hierarchy. Largely disenfranchised and undervalued, these teaching faculty are singularly associated with the revenue production that increasingly funds the enterprise, including its leadership. The debundling of faculty roles is thus directly connected to the development of a management class in higher education.

ship becomes reduced to "management" of programs and peers—a shell game that involves spreadsheets, the clever manipulation of resources, and, often, the maintenance of "no-win" labor situations and the betrayal of colleagues.

Faculty culture can allow for and even reinforce these circumstances. In 1998, Richard E. Miller warned against faculty's "willed ignorance about the bureaucratic intricacies of life in the academy"; to eschew the bureaucratic is applauded as virtuous within faculty culture, Miller observed, and rendered "a sign of elevated intelligence" (3, 9, quoted in Strickland). Faculty may refuse to come near the orbit of administration as if one might inevitably succumb to the gravity of corporatized logics—or, resisting it, might imagine oneself innocent of fraught university systems. But this disavowal—what Hugh Heclo calls "institutional distrust"—comes at great cost. Faculty distaste for the business of leading our universities has, whether consciously or not, amounted to a forfeiture of the rights and responsibilities of the faculty. The righteous unwillingness to "get one's hands dirty" with administrative work in order to preserve a "pure" space of intellectual life translates to reward structures that value certain traditional forms of research over the "service" work of university leadership from within the faculty ranks. Tenure and promotion guidelines and department processes do little to support and scaffold faculty leadership and instead impose ever heightening productivity standards against which a program or unit leader will likely be at a significant "productivity disadvantage." Administrative work pulls a person out of the classroom and leaves little focused time for research, writing and scholarship—especially as one is "on call" for the broad range of program, departmental, and university concerns.[5] Leadership work is all-encompassing, and yet it becomes shoehorned into "service" work within the unyielding requirements of the personnel file.

Turning Toward a Theory of Leadership We Can Live With

In the face of these circumstances, we seek an emancipatory vision for our leadership roles that can meet the warranted reluctance to participate in institutional neoliberalism. We argue for a leadership that works to unseat rather than reinforce the status quo. The form of leadership we envision as faculty ourselves is one that works for rather than against our own and our colleagues' personal best interests and professional standards.

---

5. These reductions in scholarly activity also impact the conversation and the thought and theory our fields can access and develop: If scholarship matters, then the absence of it matters, too. How do we measure that which does not happen within our intellectual communities when faculty are called upon to do the management of the mundane but have little time or access to address the most important decisions of the university in scholarship or in the meeting room?

We seek to reclaim an idea of leadership as the enactment of power over versus power to. Power over leads to forms of authoritarianism that reinforce hierarchy and engage in oppressive abuses of power, even when (or perhaps especially when) such abuses are subtle and nuanced. Power to involves the power to act on, to effect change, and to engage in generative power which we define as unleashing possibilities and liberating all to achieve their best hopes and dreams so that education might flourish. As faculty, especially those of us with tenure, we do have some agency and purchase within the university—the privilege of relative job security and power in our ability to collectively organize, whether we can do so officially or not, and whether we find ourselves in collective bargaining units or in right-to-work states. We also have powerful theories and understandings that equip us: We know the lie of neutrality. We know the neoliberal traps. Many faculty—especially those who have been most harmed by institutional culture—have what Sara Ahmed calls "counter-institutional knowledge of how universities work, for whom they work" (22), knowledge that is hard-won from the experience of seeking redress and accountability within university processes. Such institutional knowledge can be leveraged to instigate institutional change.

> Elected to a faculty fellowship position on advising, Janelle worked with over a dozen colleagues to collaboratively build a report that argued for significant changes to the handling and messaging of "academic probation." The report recommended moving away from the term "probation" because of its punitive connotations. While the submission of the report itself went unacknowledged by university leadership, change was realized in the months following the report, as the right people repeated the recommendations in the right conversations. A representative from Project Rebound joined the conversation, offering critical context on the term "probation" with the ethos to illuminate its harmful implications within the broader framework of a carceral society. Change happens in academic institutions through a kairotic combination of ethos and relationship. Janelle sees this example of leadership as a case study for how change-making is often non-linear, launched through relationship-building and maintained through ongoing conversations that help to change awareness and understanding over time. Change cannot always be programmed or set to a particular timeline. It happens through ramified networks and unpredictable, emergent processes. Our work is to adapt and respond to what emerges, while continuing to move with accountability and integrity. Attuning to the particular conditions of a space and finding ways to communicate compassionately and strategically in the moment is often an effective way forward.

Joddy Murray, Dean of the College of Liberal Arts at Southern Illinois University, professor of rhetoric, and former faculty senate chair, recommends a version of leadership that is tied to complexity theory, where leaders are "facilitators of connectivity, rather than … keepers of increasingly distilled expertise within specialized hierarchies or organizational charts" (513). Murray asserts that "complexity theory argues that complex organizational behavior is characterized by non-linear, emergent change; interaction and interdependency; unpredictability; autocatalytic behavior; and dynamic movement" (515) which holds promise for creating "new patterns of coherence and structures of relation" (514). Such a model reduces dependence upon charismatic or authoritative leaders while releasing the potential of "the collective over the individual" (517).[6]

With Murray, we seek a form of leadership that aligns with the ways-of-knowing and values we profess in the classroom. We see in Murray the capacity for articulating a theory of leadership that grows out of the ways we research, teach, and live. A holistic understanding of leadership can be robust enough to meet the enervating realities of the university as it stands today. A theory of leadership that we can live with will be one that promotes living and thriving in the face of dehumanizing conditions.

> We have learned recently about the U.S. Surgeon General's description of toxic workplaces as genuine threats to the health and wellness of workers and how these threats often manifest in higher education settings as bullying and disrespect (Orbe-Austin). Sue was bullied by a colleague, and departmental leadership was averse to confronting the bullying behavior. As a result, Sue decided to seek new opportunities elsewhere in her university. She now aspires to more courageous forms of leadership than were modeled for her.

We seek a theory of leadership that recognizes the whole self, including what Paul Puccio names as a "spiritual dimension…[to] all aspects of how our institutions work" (81). That spiritual dimension recognizes the necessity of contemplation, an appreciation for uncertainty, attentiveness, inner growth, patience, forgiveness. Such a model of leadership brings community members into responsibility to the community, positioning them as conscious and committed actors-in-relation who are responsible to the group and to the good of the whole. Such a theory of leadership must counter the tendencies of white supremacy culture (Okun, et al.) and instead embrace the relational and the emergent, in ways articulated by adrienne maree brown in *Emergent Strategy*. Brown's work

---

6. Murray, writing in 2017, connected this theory to the circulation of information and new formulations of authorship achieved through multiplying networks, an idea that seems to have predicted the rise of AI but perhaps could not imagine how non-authoritative multimodal authorship would become by 2025.

is guided by the famous words of Octavia E. Butler's *Parable of the Sower*, "All that you touch, you change. All that you change, changes you. The only lasting truth is change." *Emergent Strategy* guides us toward a radical acknowledgment of the deep interconnectedness that characterizes our living. The book calls us toward leadership as a living practice: fractal, tender, accountable, and awake to the impermanent and possibility of each moment. Brown views leadership as an adaptive practice that aligns with the patterns of the natural world: recognizing that all life is adaptive, nonlinear, iterative, and interdependent. Emergent strategy embraces complexity, uncertainty, and the idea that small, intentional actions can catalyze large-scale transformation.

Mindful leadership begins with the recognition that change is constant and complexity is fundamental. Leaders attuned to this reality embrace iterative, flexible, and responsive processes that hold space for multiple perspectives and needs. This approach resists rigid control and instead fosters ecologies of care, innovation, and adaptation—centered around integrity, empathy, and shared purpose. Mindful leadership is relational as it values interpersonal accountability and the cultivation of trust. Rather than rushing to resolution, mindful leadership moves slowly enough that difference can be respected and interconnectedness can be acknowledged. Mindful leadership accepts what is present, holding space for ambiguity and tension while remaining curious to the emergence of each moment. Mindful leadership embraces change and engages with it deliberately and ethically, seeing each moment as a call to evolve, to adapt with integrity, and to co-create futures that are more just, inclusive, and humane. Such an orientation also counters the illusion of permanence that so often drives institutional inertia and entrenchment.

Following the work of Beth Berila, Ruth King, Rhonda V. Magee, Zenju Earthlyn Manuel, Lama Rod Owens, Angel Kyodo Williams, and Jasmine Syedullah, we see mindful practice as foundational to an anti-oppressive orientation. A culturally sustaining theory of leadership will also be one that encourages our full participation, bringing our full, vulnerable selves to each space and encounter. In articulating such a theory of leadership, we are influenced by the theories of intersectional feminism, of antiracist practice, and of contemplative orientations to our work.[7]

As a prompt for further exploration, we offer a heuristic that simplifies, in binaristic terms, how we understand the status quo in contrast to transformational possibilities of leadership. We formatted the following as a T-table not to present a simple dichotomy, but to instead share a version of how change and redefinition can be imagined. The comparative list identifies a series of values and

---

7. See also Hinton, Mary Dana. *Leading from the Margin: College Leadership from Unexpected Places*. 1st ed., Johns Hopkins University Press, 2024.

guiding principles of leadership praxis, drawing from multiple sources of influence. We hope that this table, which represents our personal reflection, can be used and modified by others in articulating a theory of leadership. The table can prompt us to ask how a given decision is aligned with specific values—normative values that have sustained an institutional status quo or values that move the institution toward a different future. We organize the schematic with the labels of "task mind"—that term we came to as we reflected on our initial, default behavior patterns—and what we think of as mindful and relational leadership, drawing from the work of adrienne maree brown and others.

Table 1.

	TASK MIND Status Quo Maintenance	MINDFUL & RELATIONAL LEADERSHIP Transformation Toward Thriving
Precedent-Preserving vs. Community-Centered	• Preserving "the way it has been done" • Relying on precedent as default • Reacting to the immediate • Allowing defensiveness	• Valuing adaptation and responsiveness with integrity • Responding in alignment with core priorities, values and purpose • Operating from the assumption that change is constant • Considering the implications of decisions for generations to come • Being vigilant about continued complicity in institutional norms that have been exclusionary and subjugating (Stein, 2002; Kuokkanen, 2007)
Transactional vs. Humanizing	• Focusing on tasks over relationships • Insisting on input/output models	• Practicing interpersonal accountability • "Moving at the speed of trust"[8] • Promoting healing • Thwarting systems and structures of privilege to move toward justice and inclusion • Responding with empathy, respect, and care • Leading with vulnerability toward growth (allowing fallibility, emotional exposure, humility enough to learn)

---

8. This is a principle of emergent strategy. brown, adrienne maree. *Emergent Strategy: Shaping Change, Changing Worlds*. AK Press, 2017.

Paternalistic vs. Responsive	• Assuming there is a "right" answer (consistent with a paternalistic orientation)	• Inviting the complexity of decision-making and the need for multiple points-of-view • Honoring the stories and experiences of each person in the community • Valuing iterative, flexible, and experimental processes that are nuanced in response to needs
Homogenizing vs. Diverse	• Insisting on a dominant worldview or perspective • Comparing to a singular standard (deficit-based thinking)	• Committing to asset-based and growth-minded frames • Recognizing cultural wealth (Yosso) • Respecting epistemic difference (Kuokkanen) • Honoring difference and the specific needs of each person involved
Top-Down vs. Coalitional	• Maintaining a hierarchical structure • Centralizing leadership • Limiting transparency	• Holding to the principle: "Nothing about us without us is for us." Those most affected by a decision lead the decision-making • Asking at every turn: who is at the table and who is not? What voices are centered and what voices are left out?
Undermining vs. Building	• Offering critique without vision • Dismissing and denigrating what is offered in earnest	• Moving toward vision • Mediating tensions and conflicts rather than ignoring or quashing them • Offering what is constructive • Collaborating in good faith and with attention to power relations
Fear-Based vs. Possibility-Based	• Assuming a zero-sum orientation • Presuming scarcity • Creating false urgency • Trafficking in fear	• Moving with vision toward transformation • Moving slowly enough that transformation can take effect

Depleting vs. Balancing	• Maintaining an ethos and environment that promotes workaholism, over-burdening, and burnout • Allowing unclear or unreasonable standards that prompt anxiety, fear, and striving • Focusing on the individual's productivity rather than the conditions of work • Manufacturing urgency	• Taking a whole-person orientation; prioritizing mind-body intelligence • Cultivating mindful practice; increasing awareness of body, feelings, thought • Slowing down and acting from calm awareness • Cultivating whole selves in relation • Offering flexibility and respecting personal boundaries around work • Optimizing work environments to create the conditions where vision, expression, and innovation can become possible

Guided by adrienne maree brown's principles of emergent strategy we each have sought to transform our practice. We take to heart brown's recognition that "what you pay attention to grows" and we seek to bring mindful attention to the elements in our lives that contribute to thriving. Attentive to the mindful principle "how you do one thing is how you do everything," we turn to aspects of our lives outside the office as potential sites of transformation— practices that might translate back to our leadership on campus.

Nowadays, Sue is examining the leadership instincts she has lost and found, found and lost over the years by returning to something she loves, which is running. While she is not as fast as she was when her academic career began 30 + years ago, she is fortunate in that she can still put one foot in front of the other. Sometimes she walks, sometimes she hikes, sometimes she runs. When she does so, she is reminded that there is rarely a problem so big that her own movement through space doesn't provide at least provisional understanding, if not solution. Her own embodiment helps her to untangle that which defies knowing in front of a computer screen. Her surgically repaired hand reminds her of both her own vulnerability and her own strength. When she is in a meeting where there seem to be predators all around the table, she breathes deep and centers herself, all reptilian brain within a cerebral environment. She returns to what she knows deeply about how we must as humans become more responsible to each other and to the environment. All the literature in the world tells us this and the problems in our locus of control require clarity, not urgency, more understanding and judgment and less institutional logic. Even when our tendons are severed and our embodied selves compromised, we can deepen essential connections and restore the sinew of our professional and personal lives.

In 2023, Janelle stepped down from the chair position and took a sabbatical to complete yoga teacher training, with confidence that yoga philosophy and daily practice would transform her orientation to her institutional work. She is learning how steady awareness allows one to pause against the manufactured urgency of the next institutional crisis, the next call for slashing budgets, the next threat of closed programs. Non-attachment, of course, is not indifferent disengagement; it is a way of allowing each moment to teach what it teaches. Janelle seeks to lead from a place of accountability, partnership, and attentiveness to how power moves in institutions that have long perpetuated harm. She is inspired by Hollins University President Mary Hinton's advice that "most of leadership is managing yourself and your reactions to things."[9] The strength of conscious presence allows one to slow the flood of demands enough to see their implications and ramifications. Such presence is what allows us to have capacity to move forward.

We share the above heuristic as only a starting point, and we recognize that the suggestions listed above will carry different meanings for different faculty, based on identity, cultural background, and so on. We see this heuristic as an invitation for each of us to situate our own leadership philosophies in relation to the interlocutors and influences that are meaningful to us. Karen Tellez-Trujillo provides an example of how to articulate one's archive of influence: In her discussion of Feminist Leadership Practices for the journal *Peitho*, Tellez-Trujillo writes of the "polyphony of voices" that have provided the values and lessons that guide her: for example, "community listening (Fishman, Garcia, House), difference (Kerschbaum), resistance (Anzaldúa, hooks, Enoch), language and experience (Lu), writing as a feminist (Ede and Lunsford), and as a Chicana (Ruiz, Ritchie), feminist rhetorical resilience (Flynn, Sotirin, Brady), solidarity and illusions of solidarity (Mohanty, Restaino), hope (Glenn), care (Royster, Kirsch), and storytelling (Cisneros)." An important exercise is for each of us to identify our own archive in this way — and the guiding principles we find there.

Mindful leadership is a reflective and relational orientation toward institutional life that seeks not merely to manage, but to transform systems toward thriving. Mindful leadership is grounded in deep awareness of self and others, and attentive to both the interpersonal and systemic dynamics that shape our institutions. It prompts us to ask, as Roderick Ferguson does in *The Reorder of Things*, "How are modes of power exercised upon the daily lives of minoritized subjects and knowledges and how was that exercise prepared for in histories that

---

9. The quote is from the Leaders on Leadership Podcast, Academic Search, Recorded August 2023 with Jay Lemsons. https://www.academicsearch.org/blog/leaders-on-leadership-mary-dana-hinton/. See also Hinton's book *Leading from the Margins*.

are supposedly no more?" (4). And what can we do to thwart those exercises of power that maintain an oppressive status quo?

Supporting Mindful and Relational Faculty Leadership: Steps to Take

We seek a scaffolding for leadership that is actual, rather than performative. We seek the forms of structural support that would enable faculty to truly "move the needle" in the direction of principles of justice, antiracism, equity, and inclusion. In what follows we elaborate some of the supports we find necessary to address the gap in how we prepare for, and how we value, faculty leadership.

1. Embrace and build upon theories of leadership, including those in writing studies, such as Joddy Murray's work that deemphasizes the leader and accentuates leadership, "distributing power… across networks… that encourage collaboration" (522) so that a body of thought can be drawn upon as we take on these roles. Provide the specialized knowledge and the disciplinary support for faculty to become what Sara Ahmed calls "institutional mechanics" (27)—people with the knowledge of a system necessary to transform it.

2. Utilize genres that will promote self-reflection, including that of a "leadership statement" to work similarly to the teaching statement—a form of reflective writing that articulates one's philosophy and orientation to a leadership role. The leadership statement should work in tandem with the diversity statement to specify an approach to administration that is explicitly accountable to values of equity and inclusion. Such "statements" need not take traditional form but might even include poems, parables, a collage, or other genre.

3. Create communities of practice and learning communities for faculty leaders. Establish (and materially support and compensate) mentoring relationships and formal opportunities that promote knowledge-sharing, connection, and support for faculty leaders.

4. Celebrate transformational successes—i.e., those moments where a vision of a more inclusive and antiracist institution are realized. Share stories between institutional communities to offer models and meaning for our work. These forms of celebration and recognition are a counterpoint to the strong pull to maintain institutional norms. Genuine connection and care can be a compelling means of enacting systemic and cultural change.

5. Rewrite tenure and promotion guidelines to offer recognition of transformational leadership in the tenure and promotion process. This includes: reallocation of expectations for promotion as well as clear guidelines for how administrative work will be documented and represented in the file.

6. Develop a cross-institutional code of ethics for faculty leaders. The American Association of University Administrators has a Code of Ethics, but we know of no similar code that applies to faculty leaders. Building the institutional documents—Code of Ethics, Standards of Professional Practice, etc. — can help guide our work and also articulate the scope and import of our role within the university community.
7. Create the infrastructure where statements of advocacy and practice for faculty leaders can be deliberated upon and developed for their rhetorical force in supporting broader policy and decision-making within educational institutions.
8. Compile a repository of resources for faculty leaders to make relevant research and scholarship more readily accessible. Prioritize common concerns in the role in the indexing process.
9. Generate forums for active conversation and peer-to-peer mentoring and support among faculty leaders across institutions—perhaps building upon what exists within organizations such as AAC&U, AERA, ACE, Teachers for Social Justice, and so on. An active international network of faculty leaders could have the power to make statements that lead to policy change, as it could also provide the means of lobbying for greater support and material access for individuals who are most disenfranchised within institutional hierarchies and resource allocations.
10. Continue labor activism and organizing, with an understanding that faculty labor conditions are student learning conditions. Support faculty in maintaining multiple pillars of academic life, including research and teaching and flexibility to design the roles that fit their skillset and interest, with assurance of job security and compensation.

Given our institutional conditions, our argument may be read as idealistic and impractical; yet, we would argue that our orientation is fundamentally pragmatic. It is about the practical matter of how we remain relevant to the students who come to us. An inclusive, culturally responsive education is an imperative. Improved educational conditions for all students and their families is an imperative. As faculty, our scholarship helps us touch the contours of what an antiracist education can be; we need to translate that theory into practice not only inside the classroom but for the institution at large. If we continue down the current path, we are headed toward irrelevance and continued harm. We need to create cultures that people want to be part of, and that means our institutions need to change. Fostering that change requires leadership, rather than merely acquiescence to administrative tasks.

We recognize that we are questioning some of the most entrenched assumptions of our profession: about the role of the faculty member on the campus, about scope of work and responsibility, about the faculty member's relationship to the neoliberal university. We need to reorient so that we no longer see the work of leadership as a loathsome responsibility, but instead honor the responsibility and opportunity of it. This is an act of reclamation of the values we hold as educators. Indeed, our educational commitment depends on our deliberate cultivation of leadership capacity, in order to restore meaningful, deliberative participatory governance for faculty and students. We owe it to our students, who will become leaders themselves, to model a liberatory orientation to leadership, and we owe them an agentive relationship to their institution. Our work should also help forge new pathways for student leadership in the institution as well.

There is much stacked against us. The political realities we're facing in this current moment of 2025 mean that leadership today requires a fundamentally different orientation that is all the more vigilant about our obediences (whether anticipatory or enforced). We are in a moment that demands resistance, clarity, and moral courage. Our leadership practices have been formed not in stable times but in crisis after crisis. And yet, despite all this, we remain committed to imagining and enacting a better administrative life—one rooted in integrity, critical reflection, and hope.

Works Cited

Ahmed, Sara. *Complaint!*. Duke UP, 2021.
American Association of University Administrators. "Ethical Principles for College and University Administrators." 2017. https://aaua.org/wp-content/uploads/2020/11/Ethical-Principles.pdf
Boggs, Abigail, Eli Meyerhoff, Nick Mitchell, and Zach Schwartz-Weinstein. "Abolitionist University Studies: An Invitation." 2019. Web. https://abolition.university/invitation
Bousquet, Marc. "Composition as Management Science: Toward a University without a WPA." *JAC : A Journal of Composition Theory*, vol. 22, no. 3, 2002, pp. 493–526.
brown, adrienne maree. *Emergent Strategy: Shaping Change, Changing Worlds*. AK Press, 2017.
Brown, Wendy. *Undoing the Demos: Neoliberalism's Stealth Revolution*. Zone Books, 2015.
Coe, Aaron and Ravi Chinta. "The Ontology of Scholar-Administrators: Empirical Inferences from Five Senior Administrators Who Published." *The Qualitative Report*, vol. 21, no. 3, 2016, pp. 474-484. https://doi.org/10.46743/2160-3715/2016.2265
De Genova, Nicholas. "Within and Against the Imperial University: Reflections on Crossing the Line." *The Imperial University*, edited by Piya Chatterjee and Sunaima Maira, University of Minnesota Press, 2014, pp. 301-328.
Fedukovich, Casie, and Sue Doe. "Beyond Management: The Potential for Writing Program Leadership During Turbulent Times." *Reflections*, vol. 18, no. 2, 2018, pp. 87-115.

Ferguson, Roderick A. *The Reorder of Things the University and Its Pedagogies of Minority Difference*. University Of Minnesota Press, 2012.

Heclo, Hugh. *On Thinking Institutionally*. Paradigm Publishers, 2008.

Hinton, Mary Dana, and Jay Lemons. Interview: Leaders on Leadership featuring Dr. Mary Dana Hinton, President of Hollins University." *Academic Search Podcast*. Aug. 2023. https://www.academicsearch.org/blog/leaders-on-leadership-mary-dana-hinton/

Hinton, Mary Dana. *Leading from the Margins : College Leadership from Unexpected Places*. Johns Hopkins University Press, 2024.

Hoppe, Sherry L. "Spirituality and Leadership." *New Directions for Teaching and Learning* vol. 104, 2005, pp. 83-92.

Janke, Emily M."Scholar-Administrators as Change Agents. Metropolitan Universities, vol. 30, no. 3, 2019. https://journals.indianapolis.iu.edu/index.php/muj/article/view/23202/22560 https://doi.org/10.18060/23202

Kelderman, Eric. "Politics and the Pandemic Are Straining the Role of Campus Leadership." *The Chronicle of Higher Education*, October 12, 2021.

Keller, George. *Academic Strategy: The Management Revolution in Higher Education*. Johns Hopkins University Press, 1983.

Kezar, Adrianna, and Cecile Sam. "Institutionalizing Equitable Policies and Practices for Contingent Faculty." *The Journal of Higher Education* (Columbus), vol. 84, no. 1, 2013, pp. 56–87, https://doi.org/10.1353/jhe.2013.0002.

King, Ruth. *Mindful of Race: Transforming Race from the Inside Out*. Sounds True, 2018.

Klausman, Jeffrey. "Out of the Ivory Tower and Into the Brand: How the New Two-Year College Mission Shapes the Faculty-Manager." *A Critical Look at Institutional Missions*, edited by Joseph Janangelo, Parlor Press, 2016.

Kunreuther, Frances and Sean Thomas-Breitfeld. "Fewer People Want to Lead Nonprofits. What's the Answer?" *The Chronicle of Philanthropy*, January 26, 2024.

Kuokkanen, Rauna Johanna. *Reshaping the University: Responsibility, Indigenous Epistemes, and the Logic of the Gift*. UBC Press, 2007.

Lane, Jason E. "Systems Thinking for Higher Education Leaders: Solving Wicked Programs." *Inside Higher Education*, n.d.

Lam, Sue. "The Leadership Deficit: The Problem, Its Causes, and Solutions" *The APQC Blog*, 2014. https://www.apqc.org/blog/leadership-deficit-problem-its-causes-and-solutions

Lyell, Kelly. "Prioritizing Compensation: CSU's Budget Calls for 4% Tuition Hike, 5% Raise for Employees." *Coloradoan*. 5 May 2023. Lynch, Nick. "The Leadership Pipeline Crisis in Nonprofits: A Call for Action." *Forbes*, 2024.

Magee, Rhonda V. *The Inner Work of Racial Justice: Healing Ourselves and Transforming Our Communities Through Mindfulness*. Penguin Publishing Group, 2019.

Manuel, Zenju Earthlyn. *The Way of Tenderness: Awakening through Race, Sexuality, and Gender*. Wisdom, 2015.

Micciche, Laura R., and Donna Strickland. "Feminist WPA Work: Beyond Oxymorons." *Writing Program Administration*, vol. 36, no. 2, 2013, pp. 169-77.

Miller, Richard E.. *As If Learning Mattered : Reforming Higher Education*. Cornell University Press, 1998.

Murray, Joddy. "Complexity Leadership and Collective Action in the Age of Networks." *College English* vol. 79, no. 5, 2017, pp. 512-25. http://www.jstor.org/stable/44805936

Nelson, Cary. "What Hath English Wrought: The Corporate University's Fast Food Discipline." *Workplace*, 1998. https://ices.library.ubc.ca/index.php/workplace/article/view/183718

Neuroleadership Institute. "A Leadership Crisis is Emerging: Here's How to Prepare." 16 May 2023.

Okun, Tema, et al. *Characteristics of White Supremacy Culture*. Originally written and published in 1999. https://www.whitesupremacyculture.info/

Orbe-Austin, Richard. "A 10-Point Plan to End Toxic Workplaces in Higher Education." *Inside Higher Education*, 27 February 2023.

Perlmutter, David D. "Admin 101: Administrators Need Self-Care, Too." *The Chronicle of Higher Education*. 15 Oct. 2021.

Prashad, Vijay. "Teaching by Candlelight." *The Imperial University*, edited by Piya Chatterjee and Sunaima Maira, University of Minnesota Press, 2014, pp. 329-341.

Puccio, Paul. "Even Administrators Have Souls." *JAEPL: The Journal of the Assembly for Expanded Perspectives on Learning* vol. 18, no. 18, 2012. https://doi.org/10.7290/jaepl1817rl

Scott, Robert A. "Leadership Threats to Shared Governance in Higher Education,"*AAUP Journal of Academic Freedom*, vol. 11, 2020. https://www.aaup.org/JAF11/leadership-threats-shared-governance-higher-education

Simula, Brandy L. "Pursuing Your Research as a Scholar-Administrator." *Inside Higher Ed*, 20 July 2020.

Skinnell, Ryan. *Conceding Composition: A Crooked History of Composition's Institutional Fortunes*. Utah State University Press, 2016.

Sledd, James. "On Buying In and Selling Out: A Note for Bosses Old and New." *College Composition and Communication*, vol. 53, no. 1, 2001, pp. 146–49, https://doi.org/10.2307/359066

Stein, Sharon. *Unsettling the University: Confronting the Colonial Foundations of US Higher Education*. First edition. Baltimore, Maryland: Johns Hopkins University Press, 2022. Print.

Strickland, Donna. *The Managerial Unconscious in the History of Composition Studies*. Southern Illinois UP, 2011.

Tellez-Trujillo, Karen R. "Feminist Resilience at the Heart of Coalition Work." *Peitho* vol. 25, no. 4, 2023. https://cfshrc.org/article/feminist-resilience-at-the-heart-of-coalition-work

Tierney, Thomas J. "The Leadership Deficit." *Stanford Social Innovation Review*. 2006. https://ssir.org/articles/entry/the_leadership_deficit

Utz, Richard. "Against Adminspeak." *The Chronicle of Higher Education*. 24 June 2020. https://www.chronicle.com/article/Against-Adminspeak

Wenger, Christy. *Yoga Minds, Writing Bodies: Contemplative Writing Pedagogy*. WAC Clearinghouse and Parlor Press, 2015.

Williams, Angel Kyodo, Lama Rod Owens, and Jasmine Syedullah. *Radical Dharma: Talking Race, Love, and Liberation*. North Atlantic, 2016.

Zalaznick, Matt. 2022. "Higher Ed Has 7 'Wicked' Problems. Here's How Leaders Can Solve Them." *University Business*. 21 Dec. 2022 https://universitybusiness.com/higher-ed-has-7-wicked-problem-how-leaders-solve-them

CONNECTING

Bringing Mindfulness into First-Year Composition

Matthew Lemas

I first stumbled upon the relationship between mindfulness and writing sometime after college. I had been meditating for a few years—not perfectly, but enough to notice the way it softened the inner critic and procrastinator that usually accompanied me to the page.

Eventually, with a daily practice, I no longer obsessed (as much) over whether my sentences were "good enough," and wrote with far fewer conditions—less concerned with the time of day, for instance, or whether I was in a "writerly" mood. The practice didn't make writing easy, necessarily, but more possible, a habit I was willing to return to, day after day.

When I entered graduate school, and was given the opportunity to design a thematic first-year composition course as a student instructor during the fall of 2023, the choice felt obvious to me. Dubbing the class "Mindfulness Rhetorics," I wanted my students to encounter mindfulness not merely as a buzzword, but something they could integrate into their writing lives, a practice of embodied awareness, patience, and non-judgment. In effect, I wanted them to see what I had come to see—that the mind which so often derails us in writing might also be the tool that steadies us, if we learn to meet it differently.

The course unfolded in two parts. In the first five weeks, we focused on mindfulness as a lived practice: short meditations at the beginning of class led by me, reflections on the relevance of mindfulness concepts in writing, such as trust and "letting go," and a major assignment that ultimately asked them to define mindfulness for themselves, considering its relevance to their future writing life. In the second half of the semester, we turned outward, treating mindfulness as a discourse to be analyzed, exploring topics such as cultural appropriation and corporatization. But it was that opening unit—this intersection of practice and reflection—that most interested me. Could mindfulness, I wondered, potentially help students transfer what they learned in first-year composition to other writing situations?

This question was motivated by broader research on transfer I had explored at the time, which revealed how often students struggle to carry what they learn in the composition classroom into new contexts (Wardle; Yancey et al.). Concurrently, more recent work on mindfulness in higher education had suggested that contemplative practice could strengthen metacognition—the same skill that so often underlies transfer (Featherstone; Jankowski & Holas). I considered my class, then, the ideal environment to further explore this hypothesis.

To begin, I created what I called the "metacognitive essay" as their first major assignment. The prompt was simple enough: *From our readings, what does mindfulness mean to you, and how might you see mindfulness as a relevant component of your future writing life?* Students drew on *Wherever You Go, There You Are* by John Kabat-Zinn, an introductory mindfulness text, as well as *Naming What We Know*, a collection of threshold concepts edited by Linda Adler-Kassner and Elizabeth Wardle, weaving together ideas from mindfulness and writing studies, respectively, to narrate their own developing practice.

To then see what students might have carried from that initial essay, I asked them to revisit these ideas in their later rhetorical reflections throughout the semester, which were written after each subsequent major assignment (an argumentative research paper and a multimodal project of their choice). After analyzing seventeen students' essays and reflections, I discovered four themes that, to me, captured students' eagerness to transform their relationship to writing entirely, viewing mindfulness as the tool in which to do so.

In the theme of *Accepting Hardship*, for instance, students described writing struggles as part of the process, rather than as evidence of their failure. One student wrote, "A good writer is able to allow themselves room to get upset and mess up as long as they can practice and learn from experience." She linked this shift to mindfulness, which she said taught her that her headspace directly shapes her confidence on the page.

Then, under *Experiencing and Recognizing Benefits*, many students described more practical effects: improved concentration, longer writing sessions, less distraction. Nearly half explicitly said mindfulness helped them focus, often connecting that focus to better outcomes in their drafts. Others reported authenticity as a surprising benefit, claiming that mindfulness allowed their writing to sound "more like me" instead of a performance for the teacher.

Cultivating Tools was where students became more explicit about what they would take with them. "Non-judgment" and "non-doing" appeared most frequently. As one student put it, "Non-doing allows me to stop worrying about whether I'm productive enough and just be present." Another wrote, "By integrating non-judgment ... in our writing, it can enable us to be more flexible with our ideas and even promote the introspection of counterarguments." Here, students were discovering tools flexible enough for a diverse range of future writing assignments.

But it was in *Applying Practices* that students most overtly showed evidence of transferring mindfulness beyond the initial assignment. A majority said they meditated or practiced breathing before later writing tasks. One reflected: "Before starting to write I participated in breathing exercises to get myself in a stable place to write well. Writing [the metacognitive] essay made me realize how helpful it really can be." Another, who created a podcast for her multimodal project, described planning sessions around moments of mindfulness: "My brainstorming and writing turned out better if I did a mindfulness practice each time before I worked on the podcast." Indeed, her podcast was a strong one.

These weren't always dramatic breakthroughs, of course, and neither was this a perfect experiment—these students did sign up for a mindfulness-themed course, after all, which likely made them more willing to integrate these practices in the first place. However, I still felt I was onto something, that mindfulness could, even in small ways, transfer the lessons from first-year composition beyond any one assignment, or any one course.

Now—no longer a graduate student, but a part-time lecturer at Chapman— I am in my third year of teaching Mindfulness Rhetorics, and with it, my third year of assigning this essay. Has anything changed? Yes—AI, for one thing. When I first taught the course, ChatGPT had been out for less than a year, and only a handful of students had really engaged with it. Now, nearly all of them use GenAI to some degree.

That worries me, of course, for the myriad ways that are discussed near-daily in popular media—an outsourcing of process and critical thinking, for example, or an inability to handle difficult reading. However, when I teach this particular assignment today, I don't feel the despair I might were it to be, say, a rhetorical analysis, or research paper—genres I believe to have great merit, but genres that students are now more than eager to outsource to GenAI.

Rather, I find students still willing to examine the concepts and practices that embody them, that transform writing from an academic chore into an extension of their life—a life that, more and more, they are so desperate to live with awareness. That hasn't changed either when I've brought this assignment outside the confines of Chapman to more standard "English 101" courses at nearby community colleges; to quote Ram Dass, most students seem eager to "Be Here Now."

Ultimately, when I read students' metacognitive essays and subsequent reflections today, I discover something reassuring: there are certain practices that don't lose their relevance with the forward march of technological progress. If anything, they become all the more important, for—if practiced often enough, and with an openness to their effects—they can show us who we are, and why we write in the first place.

Works Cited

Adler-Kassner, L., and E. Wardle. *Naming What We Know, Classroom Edition: Threshold Concepts of Writing Studies*. Utah State University Press, 2016.

Featherstone, Jared. 'Contemplative WAC: Testing a Mindfulness-Based Reflective Writing Assignment across Courses.' *The Journal of the Assembly for Expanded Perspectives on Learning: JAEPL*, vol. 25, 2019, pp. 19–34.

Jankowski, Tomasz, and Pawel Holas. 'Metacognitive Model of Mindfulness.' *Consciousness and Cognition*, vol. 28, 2014, pp. 64–80, https://doi.org10.1016/j.concog.2014.06.005.

Kabat-Zinn, Jon. *Wherever You Go, There You Are: Mindfulness Meditation in Everyday Life*. Hyperion, 2005.

Wardle, Elizabeth. 'Understanding "Transfer" from FYC: Preliminary Results of a Longitudinal Study.' *WPA Writing Program Administration: Journal of the Council of Writing Program Administrators*, vol. 31, no. 1–2, 2007, pp. 65–85.

Yancey, K. B., et al. *Writing across Contexts: Transfer, Composition, and Sites of Writing*. Utah University Press, 2014.

A VIEW FROM THE CONFERENCE

The Giving and the Receiving: Spiritual Traditions and Teaching, AEPL Summer Conference 2025, Estes Park, CO.

Conference Organizers: Laurence Musgrove and Joonna Smitherman Trapp

Writing Our Spiritual Autobiographies

Editor's note: This past year, AEPL held its first full, in-person conference since the pandemic at our beloved Estes Park location in the Rockies. To commemorate the return of this staple event for our organization, here's a snapshot of one of the workshops, led by immediate past AEPL Chair, Geraldine DeLuca, "Writing Our Spiritual Autobiographies," in which DeLuca asked attendees to consider, where and how did we begin, spiritually? What sustains us now? DeLuca provided three prompts by Wallace Stevens, Karen Armstrong, and Audre Lorde to aid attendees in their reflection and writing processes. These prompts appear at the end of this section.

My Dad's Playful God

Bhushan Aryal

In June 2025, on a bright summer morning in Estes Park, Colorado— in the lap of the mountains, like the Himalayas of my childhood— Geraldine DeLuca asked us, the workshop participants, to write our spiritual biographies.

She said,

"Think of a formative spiritual experience you remember, and write about that."

The assumption was clear: we were all spiritual beings, each holding something tender in the caverns of memory, waiting to be excavated and brought to light.

Everyone began to write— we would soon have to share our stories.

Here is what I wrote:

I remember my father reading *Krishna-Charitra*,
that old, revered family book, a sacred abode for gods.

Inside our hillside house in western Nepal, not far from Resunga, Ruru, and Lumbini— lands long enchanted by seekers and saints— he would read by fireside on cool evenings after dinner.

My siblings, my mother, and I gathered close, listening as he recited the poetic lines.

Stories of Krishna's mischievous boyhood, his fearless heart and quiet wisdom— a child-god who danced, teased, and guided.

My father's unique voice, hovering between epic poetry and village song, held us still in wonder.

Though the stories were serious, the telling was never severe.

Laughter sat beside reverence, like Krishna himself hiding in the reeds.

Now I am a father, with teenage sons and a face that mirrors his.

I've devoured books upon books, listened to sacred chants and philosophical debates, read sermons, sutras, songs.

On my bookshelf sit the *Bhagavad Gita*, the *Dhammapada*, the *Bible*, and the lyrical Sufi sermons.

They do not argue with one another. Though some may fight in their names, to me they are not contradictions— only different versions, different degrees of the same longing.

All point to spirit.
All pulse with light.

And perhaps that light comes from the god my father offered— a playful god, and the joyful, loving storyteller who gave him voice.

Books: My Paths to Spirituality

Beverly Brannan

Books were my first path to spirituality. They whisked me with words, images, and ideas to new worlds, new people, and new ways of thinking and being. They allowed me to live in different countries, understand strange cultures, and people; they allowed me to dwell there, dream there, to be alive and breathe there, to touch, smell, hear, and see worlds I had never imagined. They were a spiritual place for me. They transformed me

Peace fills me when I read. I follow paths that lead me to new religions, new ways of thinking about life's big questions, and the small questions as well. I trace new roads to strange worlds both real and fictional. I travel to the past and to the future, to places real and imagined. I am an explorer.

My father recognized my love of reading as a child and he encouraged me. He had bookcases built into by bedroom walls and allowed me unlimited access to any books I wanted to read. Mythology, history, poetry, fairy tales and novels lined my bookcases. As a young girl, I discovered Nancy Drew and joined the Nancy Drew Book Club. I waited excitedly each month for the two new mystery novels to arrive in the mail. Nancy Drew introduced me, a young girl in the early 1960s, to a world where women were self-assured, and adventurous. They didn't follow the mid-century rules about the way that young women were supposed to behave. Nancy Drew introduced me to feminism and to the spirituality of strong and brave women.

I lean into books for peace, strength, and knowledge. They led me to my interest in Buddhism. When I was very young, I read Herman Hesse's *Siddhartha*, and through the years I have read it again and again. It became the first step on a longer path to more books about Buddhism that have changed my way of thinking and being. Those books include *The Art of Happiness* by his Holiness the Dalai Lama and Howard C. Cutler and *The Art of Living* by Thich Nhat Hanh. They led to my implementing Buddhist beliefs into my life.

Although not a traditional book on meditation and Buddhism, Twyla Tharp's *Keep It Moving: Lessons for the Rest of Your Life* has given me wonderful insights on how to use meditation and movement to cure the fear of the aging process. She taught me how to live a life of purpose no matter my age. She taught me that dance is a form of meditation. It liberates the body and mind to experience the joys of being alive. When we dance, we celebrate our bodies and our souls. We become aware of the wondrous gift that living is.

Reading itself is a type of meditation for me. Books take me into a different realm, both physically and mentally, one where my problems fade, where my mind and body relax and become peaceful. Books lead me to understand, sympathize, and experience more love both towards the people I know and those I have never met. They show me that there isn't one universal truth or way to love. They give me self-forgiveness and assist me in forgiving others as well.

If Twyla Tharp taught me to move, Alan Lightman taught me to waste time. A physicist and novelist at MIT, Lightman's books, *In Praise of Wasting Time* and *The Transcendent Brain: Spirituality in the Age of Science,* made me realize that "wasting time" and reconnecting with nature are essential to our mental, emotional, and creative well-being. We need spaces in our day to let our mind wander so that we may make new discoveries about ourselves and the wondrous natural world that surrounds us. He reminds us to take walks and rediscover that nature can heal our minds and souls.

Because of books, I'm never alone in life. They're my beloved friends and guides. They don't judge or condemn me when I make mistakes. Instead, they lead me to become a better person, more understanding of others, more patient, kinder. They teach me always, always to stay open to new people, to grab life and live it, to laugh and dance and make new friends. They teach me not to fear life, but to see it as sacred, a place filled with pages and pages of new adventures, ideas, friends, and to embrace a spirituality of goodness for all.

Tale of an Italian American Buddhist

Geraldine DeLuca

My first memory is of the priest's back. He is facing the altar, wearing an iridescent white vestment and he is holding up the Eucharist. People get up from their seats to kneel at the altar to receive communion. I leave my seat and kneel beside them.

The priest puts the host on my tongue, and I let it dissolve in my mouth. I say to myself, "My Lord and My God."

God was everywhere, I was told, and he knew everything. He was in my head, and he could hear me. Was it God the father or Jesus who was listening? Jesus was certainly the more compassionate of the two, but what must he think of my paltry, shameful thoughts?

The nuns at Wednesday afternoon catechism told us that if our parents didn't go to mass on Sunday, they would burn in hell for all eternity.

"Oh, for crying out loud," said my mother. "Religion is for children," said my father. He was reading Bertrand Russell.

So why was I going to catechism? To church? For the family. *La Famiglia.* For my Italian grandmother, for my father's religious sister. For the girls' white communion dresses and veils, for the boys' tiny blue suits. For the godmothers in their dresses and high heels, for the photographs outside the church where everyone smiled. For the ice cream cake in the afternoon.

All of this had its place, but still, if I embraced it, I would live with the flames of Hell flickering around me. Eventually, at age 15, I let go. I cut mass. My cousin and I went to a soda fountain and drank egg creams. We kept a pack of cigarettes hidden behind a table and smoked together for an hour. One day, my Uncle Tony saw us walking along Bay Parkway when we should have been in church. He told my mother, but what could she say? She wasn't in church either. And my Uncle Tony was a bitter man. He made everybody miserable. My mother knew that.

II

As a young adult, I sat next to people in my department who I knew had a spiritual practice, and I would wonder, how could these smart people believe? What did they believe in? Did they really believe in Jesus, whoever he was?

III

Years later, I discover Karen Armstrong and this passage: "Faith [is] not about belief but about practice. Religion is not about accepting twenty impossible propositions before breakfast but about doing things that change you. It is a moral aesthetic, an ethical alchemy. . ." (*The Spiral Staircase,* 2004). It is taking responsibility for your body, your mind, your behavior. It is "First do no harm."

Eventually, I go to yoga classes. I remember sitting in my yoga class, resting between poses, relaxed in my body, or my "body/heart/mind" as some of my Buddhist friends like to say, and wishing that my students could feel that way: if they could learn to take stock of their physical and spiritual condition; feel their feelings, without being overwhelmed by their families and their teachers and their part-time or even full-time jobs.

At the beginning of yoga class, we meditated for five minutes. At the end of class, we lay on the floor in *Savasana*, resting pose. We bowed to the teacher and to each other and said *Namaste*. With dignity, we rolled up our mats. This was not about God. It was about a community of people committing to caring for themselves and one another, noticing how they felt, respecting their minds, their communities.

From yoga I moved to weekly meditation—and then I became a member of a Buddhist sangha. I learned about the Three Jewels: the *Buddha*—who was not a god but a smart and curious man who left his palace of privilege to discover that we are all subject to sickness, aging, and death. His insights became the *Dharma*, or the teachings; and his followers became the *Sangha*, or the community. "Life," said the Buddha, "is full of suffering, full of a pervasive sense of dissatisfaction." And why do we suffer? Because we are subject to greed, hatred, and delusion. We spend our lives battling our desires, burnishing our image, looking for power over others. Over and over, we need to let go. "No self; no problem," said the monk. Big smile. Let go.

And so I notice: I am jealous, I feel worthless, I resent that other person. But I can let it go. Let it go. All of us in the sangha come to understand this. We don't always conquer our suffering, but we recognize that there is a path. I learn the *Brahma Viharas*: the "Four Immeasurables": loving kindness; compassion; joy in the good fortune of others; and equanimity—sitting calmly with what cannot be changed—which doesn't mean being acquiescent, but just not losing one's mind.

I learn to meditate. Sometimes I am peaceful; sometimes restless; sometimes I forget what I'm doing there. It's all part of the experience. I keep sitting. Keep breathing. Ah, how angry I feel; ah, how lonely; how fearful. I send love to those I love and to those I don't.

I smile at strangers in the street. I have a weekly meeting with other aging people. We talk about illness and death. It is okay to die. I read the newspaper, which is filled with stories of unbearable suffering. The thought of such suffering terrifies and enrages me. I do what I can, which, I understand, will never be enough. I keep sitting. I listen to others.

I have a spiritual life that I can fully embrace. "And it will take me home."

On Welcome

Nate Mickelson

The Bible I was given on my confirmation included full-color illustrations of Old and New Testament stories. The pictures were printed on thick glossy paper in clusters separated from the stories themselves. I remember one image per story, though they may have been arranged more like short comic strips. The pictures kept me company during Sunday services, especially during Reverend Miller's sermons, which, as a confirmed member of the congregation, I no longer had permission to bypass downstairs in the nursery. At twelve, fifteen minutes of one person talking seemed endless.

Church was an essential routine in my family. We attended every week, first Sunday school, then the service, then coffee after, at the Berta A. Penny United Methodist Church in Kemmerer, WY (population 3,000 and shrinking; elevation 7,000 feet). My father read from the Gospel and helped make pancakes on Mother's Day. My mother played the piano and organized Vacation Bible School in the summer. We sat in the same pew each week, surrounded by the same people, wearing "sprucy" Sunday clothes, as my mom called them—nice, but not elaborate.

I'll get back to my Bible, but it's important to first explain what it felt like to be part of the church community. There were thirty people on busy Sundays, maybe fifty for the Christmas pageant and Easter egg hunt. Similarly sized groups of Lutherans, Episcopalians, Evangelical Free parishioners and Baptists had their services nearby. A larger group of Catholics and a much larger group of Mormons met across town. Inside our yellow brick sanctuary, we knew one another every which way. No one pried but everyone listened. We smiled a lot. Some of my teachers attended, kids I knew from school but wouldn't have called friends, families that had less than mine and at least one that had a lot more.

All of this is to say that the church was a community. It was always there, and the people who made it up were always there, too. There must have been disagreements and pressures, but they didn't register. There must have been guilt and shame and sin and discomfort, too, but they haven't lasted. Neither has the religion, really, apart from some of the stories and the occasions they provided for people to come together.

I remember the feeling of looking at two pictures in my confirmation Bible, in particular. In one, Joseph is looking up from the well at his brothers plotting and eating around the edge, using his bright coat as a picnic blanket. Joseph's clothes are torn and dirty. He looks scrawny down in the well, but his face is bright. In the other picture, Samson is destroying a temple. He's shirtless, extremely muscular, bleeding from the eyes. He'll die with the rest as soon as the pillars collapse.

Joseph and Samson are the heroes of their stories. Their suffering anticipates Christ's, I've since learned, and their redemptions—Joseph's when he forgives his brothers and Samson's when he sacrifices himself—model human capacities. At twelve, I'm not sure I was so concerned with suffering or redemption or forgiveness. Instead, I was an anxious, husky, gay kid, bored in church, and attracted to pictures of two beautiful men. Joseph and Samson kept me company. My parents must have seen me "reading" their stories while Reverend Miller spoke. Lots of people in the church must have noticed I was queer, too. But no one asked, and no one drew attention to my weight or anxiety or any other difference, either.

I think it's unlikely that the congregation would have embraced me had I been more open about my desire. As caring as we were, there were limits I was staying within by remaining closeted in the ways I did. I'm sorry for the chances I missed to be more visible. All the same, the church gave me Joseph and Samson when they gave me my Bible. They also gave me the routine of community. To put it more directly, they welcomed me into a practice of being together where everyone's being there, however they were, mattered for everyone else.

An Anti-Spiritual Autobiography

Laurence Musgrove

I make no claim to originality
in the causes and the effects
of my devotion to fear, but
among the evidence you may
recognize is the comfort I find
in the solo activities of reading,
writing, observing, listening,
standing dark in conversation,
letting others have the floor,
nodding, agreeing, perhaps
offering a joke or wisecrack,
a quick form of ego display
to assure others I'm harmless,
because even fear has a thirst
for ego, big on isolating itself
from conflict and worry,
desirous of safe friendships,
which, while few, can be lasting
because once the fearful know
where safety is and the brave
hang out, they will visit often,
drink in the shine of brighter spirits.

Divinity in Nature: Peace in Presence

Kristin Rajan

For as long as I can remember, I believed in something higher than me, something bigger than me. How could I not? I grew up by the ocean. I visited mountains. I spent a lot of time sitting in trees. I saw butterflies, hummingbirds, cardinals. I would often stare directly into a dragon fly's eyes for what felt to be an infinity. (I do this whenever I can. Try it! It will blow your mind.)

Seeing the beauty surrounding me, nature was where I found the divine.

My parents divorced when I was eight years old, and I spent Sundays with Dad. He would take me to a different place of worship on our day together: churches, synagogues, temples—a myriad of religious gatherings for the year of Sundays he spent seeking both faith and solace. I think he was looking for something to believe in. I confess (because this seems a safe space for confession), I didn't want to go to those places on our Sundays together. I would have preferred to go to the beach or the woods. But I found a common thread in those religious institutions we visited. Within those different walls, I felt love, compassion, connection.

But I felt these elements most when sitting in a tree, or by a lake, or walking on the seashore. Outside of any walls, I felt most connected to something higher AND connected to everyone, seen and unseen. In nature, I felt peace, love, joy, freedom. Like the tree, I was rooted, yet bending with winds. Nature taught me to flow with change, to release my grasp. Nature comforted me during my parents' divorce and taught me gratitude that my father shared his search for consolation.

Nature consistently sustained me.

Later, as I read about different spiritual traditions, I was drawn to Buddhism. I was not surprised to learn that Siddhartha Gautama found enlightenment beneath a tree. Seeking the peace he felt under the apple tree of his youth, he sought the tree again to find peace from his suffering as an adult. Under the Bodhi tree, he realized that he was not alone in his suffering. He connected to others through his presence with the tree. The tree taught release, detachment, the path to peace.

I believe the tree was key to the Buddha's enlightenment.

I believe nature is key to our enlightenment as well. Nature teaches us release—to let go of fear, anxiety, sadness, depression, which often stem from ego and a movement away from the present, a movement into constructed stories of self and others, many delusory and destructive. I suppose nature teaches us MOST to be present, and in the present there is peace.

Nature is the peace of storylessness.

Now, I think my view on spirituality has moved from believing in something greater than me to believing that greater force is within me, always accessible. I think each moment offers an opportunity to turn within and tap peace, love, connection—all lessons from nature. I feel I am an extension of nature. I am one with the tree. My spirituality is not doctrine or preaching. It's simply be-ing.

This spirituality is about recognizing and respecting life surrounding and within—feeling gratitude for all the gifts of this journey, the beautiful and even the painful, which teach the most.

This spirituality is enriching, not depleting. Accepting, not judging. Loving, not hating.

Nature is my higher force, teaching me again and again to be present. And in this presence, I feel love, compassion, connection. My spirituality is nature—within me, around me. When I am still, I breathe into the divine.

Resiliency vs. Uncertainty

Adrian Matt Zytkoskee

In my twenties, I worked a sketchy job with an old leathery man called Hollywood. No one would tell me how he earned this nickname, but they weren't shy in describing him as "son of a bitch" who was "meaner than a wet panther." Apparently, he'd survived a war, a short stint in prison, and the death of his wife. Since that time, he'd pretty much alienated all family and friends with anger and vindictiveness. One evening when Hollywood was over an hour late returning from a task in the forest, the foreman remarked, "I'm not worried. Nothing can kill that guy . . . he's resilient as hell!"

Something about this statement bothered me at the time but, honestly, it wasn't until recently when talking with my friend Bill that I recalled the description of Hollywood as "resilient" and finally understood why I'd been bothered. Bill had said, "You know, people often think of resilience as 'grit' or toughing out hardships in silence. In my opinion, resilience is asking for help and learning to rely on whatever resources are available. It's a practice not a destination." Hollywood hadn't been resilient; he'd been mean, miserable, and stubborn.

After this revelation, I asked myself why resilience has been on my mind? The answer is because I need it right now. Life has felt hard. An emotional grind. Don't get me wrong, I have an abundance of blessings, and my problems are high-end compared to many, but this doesn't change the fact that I'm living beneath a blanket of uncertainty on many levels (personal and global). And, as we know, uncertainty can be incredibly stressful. In fact, research has demonstrated that facing possible pain is far more stressful than facing known pain. So, I've been attempting to practice resilience in a few ways.

First, I share my struggles with people I trust: a counselor (which I recognize is an incredible privilege), a close buddy, my lovely spouse, my parents, even a colleague who I know will understand. I've felt some relief after each of these conversations and, often times, they share their own struggles. As a result, I feel less alone. Less broken.

Another move I've been practicing is acceptance. Before she died from cancer, my friend Emily gave me a bracelet with the words *shikata ga nai* engraved on it. This Japanese expression means, "It cannot be helped" and is used to describe a type of deep acceptance that helps preserve dignity in the face of unavoidable tragedy or injustice. For Emily, it did not mean that she was okay with having cancer. Not at all. But she accepted that it was what it was and that beyond taking measure to treat it, she could not change reality. Though I am in NO way comparing my situation to Emily's, I find acceptance of what is—even when I greatly dislike it—to be relieving. I don't have to like something to accept that it is what has to be faced . . . that it cannot be helped.

Also in my twenties, I worked for a Jewish woman in her late eighties who'd survived a Nazi concentration camp as a young girl and had gone on to devote her life to helping others heal from trauma. Unlike Hollywood, she seemed always to be laughing, and people adored her. I asked her once how she had managed to stay so grounded. In her slight German accent, she smiled and replied, "First of all, I'm not always grounded. But there are two things I've consistently done that help immensely. I find purpose in helping others, which often keeps the hamsters out of my head. The second is that I've always found ways of blowing off steam and having fun even in tough times." Reflecting back on this conversation, I realize now just how good her advice was—wisdom that's been echoed in a lot of research (e.g., people with purpose tend to live longer). I've discovered that the more oriented I am to being of service to others (whether professionally or personally), the less time I spend worrying about myself.

I've also grown resilience through blowing off steam and having fun. I could tell you about the more traditional ways I go about this such as taking long hikes with my dog, practicing martial arts, and even screaming into a pillow when I reach the red zone. But I'd rather tell you about taking my kids to Tournament of Kings, a Las Vegas dinner show that involved medieval characters battling on horses and an array of fantastic explosions. For over an hour, we ravaged our meals like ruffians and cheered and jeered and laughed. I hadn't expected to enjoy it so much, but as we strolled out afterward—my voice hoarse from taunting—I realized how much I'd needed a break from being a responsible adult. I'm not "prescribing" a Las Vegas show for resilience, but you get the idea.

Another resiliency practice is the one I struggle with most: physical health. When I'm eating cleanly (foods not full of preservatives and that don't destroy my gut), exercising daily, avoiding excesses of (or abstaining from) alcohol, and getting solid sleep, I function better. No doubt. It's a simple concept, yet far from easy to apply, particularly when "having fun" and/or temporarily escaping pain conflicts with "bodily care." Fortunately, every day provides a new opportunity for me to try again.

Last, though far from least, is spirituality. This is a tricky one to discuss because its shape and essence vary so radically from person to person. For me, it's helpful to make spirituality a type of practice through regular meditations (sound healing is my "jam"), prayers, intentional journaling, and even reaching out to people I know could use support. I also write and talk (even out loud sometimes) to people in my life who have passed away. I'm hesitant to share this, but the truth is that it grounds me. A lot.

Another truth is that, on any given day, I might do all these things OR none of them—which is why resilience is a practice and not a "perfect." It takes effort and sometimes my efforts are far better than others (laughably so).

Ultimately, nothing I do is going to erase uncertainty from my life. It's part of the human experience. But how I cope with it can improve through practicing resiliency.

Writing Prompts

Wallace Stevens, "The Snow Man," Poetry Magazine, *1921*

One must have a mind of winter
To regard the frost and the boughs
Of the pine-trees crusted with snow;

And have been cold a long me
To behold the junipers shagged with ice,
The spruces rough in the distant glitter

Of the January sun; and not to think
Of any misery in the sound of the wind,
In the sound of a few leaves,

Which is the sound of the land
Full of the same wind
That is blowing in the same bare place

For the listener, who listens in the snow,
And, nothing himself, beholds
Nothing that is not there and the nothing that is.

Karen Armstrong, The Spiral Staircase. *Anchor Books, 2004*

Hyam Maccoby . . . told me that in most traditions, faith was not about belief but about practice. Religion is not about accepting twenty impossible propositions before breakfast, but about doing things that change you. It is a moral aesthetic, an ethical alchemy. If you believe in a certain way, you will be transformed. The myths and laws of religion are not true because they conform to some metaphysical, scientific, or historical reality but because they are life enhancing. They tell you how human nature functions, but you will not discover their truth unless you apply these myths and doctrines to your own life and put them into practice. The myths of the hero, for example, are not meant to give us historical information about Prometheus or Achilles—or for that matter, about Jesus or the Buddha. Their purpose it to compel us to act in such a way that we bring out our own heroic potential.

Audre Lorde. "Poetry Is Not a Luxury," Sister Outsider: Essays and Speeches. 1984; 2007.

As [our feelings and the honest exploration of them] become known and accepted to ourselves, they become sanctuaries and fortresses and spawning grounds for the most radical and daring of ideas, the house of difference so necessary to change. . . . Right now, I could name at least ten ideas I would have once found intolerable or incomprehensible and frightening, except as they came after dreams and poems. This is not idle fantasy but the true meaning of "it feels right to me." We can train ourselves to respect our feelings, and to discipline (transpose) them into a language that matches those feelings, so they can be shared. And where that language does not yet exist, it is our poetry which helps to fashion it. Poetry is not only dream or vision, it is the skeleton architecture of our lives.

BOOKS

Is it Just Me?

Curt Porter

Scholarship is notoriously slow.

A new academic book is usually the result of years of research, writing, review, and revision. Reading it, digesting it, and responding to it takes significant time and energy as well. All things considered, years can pass between a moment of insight and the moment that insight becomes part of a larger conversation. It's important to recognize a sort of humility that's baked into the process. Academic writers are a careful bunch. To assert that something is 'true' requires extensive debate and constant adjustment and qualification. The whole thing can be exhausting. But we do it with the goal of exploring a given problem as deeply as possible and with the hope of playing a small part in developing our always-imperfect knowledge.

In 2025, not everyone is as patient or as trusting in this process as the initiated. By all accounts, we are living in a time of social, economic, political, and ecological instability. In just the past several months popular media has reported on major cuts to medical research, massive layoffs in the public sector, dramatic changes in health guidelines, the deployment of military troops in US cities, government shutdown.... Commentators speak of the erosion of checks and balances, environmental disaster, a collapse of democratic systems. I do my best to keep up. I make mental notes to follow up with every crisis, but a new headline always comes along, and my attention shifts again. In every case, I know I'm only getting a part of the picture. And yet the media-sphere constantly promises the next big piece of the next big story. So I click and I click. I'm looking for something definitive—some sort of perspective or answer that brings everything together. It's only natural to seek out answers, and the careful deliberation of academic research isn't really designed to keep up.

I recently found myself in stunned silence at yet another batch of headlines. In this case, a conservative activist known for holding rallies on college campuses was shot and killed. It was especially salient to me because this person had visited my own campus several years before, and along with his organization had caused quite a stir. In the wake of his visit, close friends and colleagues of mine received personal threats. There were rumors of students secretly recording lectures and making professor blacklists. Faculty meetings morphed into emergency planning / group therapy sessions. Armed security was stationed outside of my department office. At one point, a bullet was found in one of our classrooms. Our administration insisted there was no credible threat, but they weren't very convincing.

I had a lot of complicated reactions when I heard about the shooting. I thought about this man's young children. I thought about my own two children and what it might be like for them to hear that their father had been shot. I thought about the idea of free speech—his and mine. I thought about the blurry lines between speech and action. I thought about the possibility and the fear of speaking candidly about all this with my students. I thought a lot about that bullet that was found in a classroom in my building.

As if on cue, a video popped up on my YouTube page. It was a familiar face. A clean-shaven and shaggy-haired guy picking a guitar outside. I knew that the viral folk-singer Jesse Welles would write a song about the shooting. He seems to have a song for every major issue and event of the past year or so. But this was fast... less than 24 hours after the fact. I clicked immediately. It was a simple little folksong that spoke to contradictions in our collective reactions to the shooting, further division and potential consequences, and an underlying vulnerability that feels both personal and social. To be fair, it wasn't Shakespeare or Dylan. I suppose it struck me so intensely because it felt like an independent voice that was uneasy with the self-righteous anger and pre-baked explanations already beginning to swirl. It was as if Welles was taking us through his own desperate search for a trustworthy compass and that he had momentarily found it in the acknowledgment of our shared mortality.

It's the immediacy of it all that brings me back to the book reviews in this issue. No one would mistake a two-minute folk song for a major research project. But I think part of what I find so important about Welles' music is that it offers up-to-the-minute commentary that rejects hackneyed partisan talking points. It comes from a place of genuine uncertainty and gives a snapshot of the process through which the artist is responding. In this way, I think his art isn't so different from good scholarship.

Each of the reviews in this issue of *JAEPL* focus on a book that was published long before this particular crisis. The books span very different academic fields and very different research methodologies. Yet each reviewer gives a glimpse of how the research behind each book emerged from lived challenges and illustrates how that research sheds light on the daily work and daily struggle that we collectively face. Kelly Sauskojus reviews *Evangelical Writing in a Secular Imaginary* (Cope), a rigorous study of religious identity as it emerges in college writing classrooms. Sauskojus emphasizes important methodological contributions of this book but does so within a nuanced discussion of the elevated power and politics surrounding religion in our public life. We get a practical lens that allows any instructor to recognize the complex process of navigating faith during a time when religion has been so fiercely politicized. The next review responds to *Curriculum Fragments,* by Tom Poetter. The book is an autobiographical work that describes and demonstrates the role of stories in education and in life.

Joseph Wiederhold takes up Poetter's invitation/challenge to work with our stories through an examination of his own. Rather than a traditional review, we see an enactment of Poetter's *currere* methodology. The result is an account of the struggle against cynicism and his desire to maintain a sense of meaning, connection, and openness in his work. I personally found myself nodding along as he described the reality of AI simulated text interrupting the possibility of genuine learning and connection through human thought and writing. I get the sense that our task is not so much a matter of identifying 'correct' or 'acceptable' uses of AI but of demonstrating to our students and to ourselves what it is we are trying to preserve when we limit its role. Wiederhold and Poetter both suggest that hope can be found in our own stories and the stories of others. Our third piece reviews *Literacies in Times of Disruption* by Bronwyn Williams. Ashna Singh provides an overview then outlines theoretical tools for recognizing the individual and collective impacts of the Covid pandemic on the literacies and the lives of college students. The review includes impressions of pandemic life that will feel familiar to many of us, and Singh offers a potent reminder that the implications and the impacts of the pandemic are still with us. More importantly, Singh also draws out a set of concepts that elaborate on the ongoing disruptions on students' individual, interpersonal, and material worlds and serve as a practical mechanism of understanding, empathy, and action.

While these three books are pretty recent by academic standards, no one would expect them to address this mornings' round of headlines and talking points. But the reviews that follow offer a glimpse of teacher-scholars engaging deeply with research and putting it in conversation with our day-to-day. Individually, they speak to the complicated role of religion in the identities of college writers, impacts of AI generated text on the relationships we seek to build through writing, and the role of emotional well-being on the literate lives of students. Taken together these reviews nudge towards an understanding of the complexity of students' lives and of connecting with them as citizens and as people. This sort of connection is something that I struggle with and strive towards in my own teaching. For whatever reason, my impression is that my students appreciate these efforts more so than in years past. That's just a feeling. I have no way to substantiate it. But similar sentiments on the part of these three reviewers have me wondering if maybe I'm not alone. I feel appreciative of these interactions with research. I feel appreciative of the researchers who have continued to put in the time and care to write books that provide foundations for these feelings, and I feel deeply thankful for the impetus to continue my own academic journey.

Works Cited

Welles, J. (2025, September 11). *Charlie* [Video]. YouTube. https://www.youtube.com/watch?v=UCBkt5Nt1wo

Cope, Emily M. *Evangelical Writing in a Secular Imaginary: The Academic Writing of Christian Undergraduates at a Public University.* Routledge, 2024, 184 pages.

Kelly Morgan Sauskojus
Clemson University

Emily Murphy Cope's *Evangelical Writing in a Secular Imaginary: The Academic Writing of Christian Undergraduates at a Public University* (2024) empirically considers how evangelical students negotiate their identities in their academic writing. Cope's project contributes to a long conversation about how composition teachers ought to respond when religion shows up in undergraduate student writing, particularly when it is evangelical or otherwise-conservative Christian rhetoric that has the potential to be disruptive or harmful (Dively; Rand; Thomson-Bunn; Vander Lei). Much of that early teacher research is highly anecdotal and considers it as axiomatic there is no place for religious rhetoric in academic writing or speech; however, a more recent strain of argument has countered that evangelical and otherwise religious students can and do productively use their faith as a rhetorical resource in academic writing and beyond (Pugh; Ringer, Vernacular; Ringer, Working). Despite that pre-Trump optimism, though, there is still an ongoing need to address legitimate concerns over the rhetoric of evangelical students, as well as calls for pedagogical practices accounting for their backgrounds (Mannon and Pivott), at least in part because evangelicals and evangelical rhetoric are at new levels of public visibility and power under Trump's second term.

First, Cope's study represents an enormous methodological contribution to the study of religion in undergraduate student writing. In a field perhaps overpopulated with anecdotes, counter-anecdotes, and small case studies, Cope approaches her research with empirical excellence, explaining with detail her data collection, coding practices, and how she arrived at final themes (an early excerpt from this research appeared in the methodologically-demanding *Research in the Teaching of English*). By positioning herself as a "Christian researcher," allowing the students she interviews to self-select as evangelical, and getting a much larger group of participants than past studies, Cope produces findings remarkable for their depth and diversity. Furthermore, this study makes a methodological contribution by offering a nuanced and productive way of considering undergraduate identity; social identity complexity theory creates a framework for how socially-constructed identities like "evangelical" or "academic" "are experienced by students and how they "constrain or capacitate academic writing and rhetorical development" (23). Given that religion as an identity category has not been theorized as robustly as, say, gender or race in writing studies, I anticipate that this theorization will be productive for researchers working on any religious community.

Cope presents longitudinal findings on how evangelical students work "within the constraints (as they perceived them) of academic writing–obscuring, compartmentalizing, and integrating faith" (5). She shows how all three of these approaches are shaped by the secular imaginary, a term she deploys from Catholic philosopher Charles Taylor to describe the culture young evangelicals share with other college students, where religion is positioned as a private and personal choice and where public, communal action and discourse assume "supernatural phenomena do not exist or are irrelevant" (14). In this framework, both evangelical students and their college writing appear "secular-while-religious".

One group of students she interviewed takes the obscuring approach, often writing about hot-button political issues that they perceive as grounded in their faith while playing by the "rules of the secular imaginary," avoiding explicitly grounding their arguments in religion (61). Many such students see the research and writing process as a way to proclaim mainstream evangelical positions on issues like abortion, recycle research from past projects, or mimic the legal and scientific rationalizations that larger conservative political organizations use, while often unsuccessfully hiding the evangelical roots of their positions.

The second group of students takes the compartmentalizing approach to negotiating academic and evangelical identities. Even though most evangelicals theoretically argue against the bifurcation of religious discourse and public/academic discourse, many students, in their everyday writing, accept it, "experiencing their faith as either relevant or appropriate only in specific domains of life" (71). Some students report writing in favor of positions they do not actually hold because they just want to succeed at the academic writing game; other students who have to write about issues like evolution rhetorically distance themselves from their findings, like the student who consistently wrote that "scientists believe" certain evolutionary facts (86).

The final writing trend that Cope identifies in undergraduate students (and this was, significantly and perhaps surprisingly, the largest group of students represented) is students who take the integrating approach to academic and evangelical identities. They see their academic writing as working toward values and goals that are shared across their evangelical and academic communities, like pursuing a career in psychology to help fight mental illness; and prioritize enacting faith values in their writing rather than explicitly naming them. For example, a cishet white male evangelical student reports that for him being a Christian means enacting love wherever he goes, and so he repeatedly uses his academic writing to learn about and disrupt Christian-led discrimination of the LGBTQ+ community on his campus. Because so many researchers expect to identify evangelical student writing by explicit mentions of faith or departure from academic norms, students in this third group have remained "largely invisible" in scholarship on the typical Christian college writing student (148). I find this last finding to be particularly indicative of the need for empirical research directly centering student perspectives and motivations for their writing, rather than relying on what is made obvious in student work or classroom interactions.

Cope concludes by offering several useful takeaways from this research, not least of which are the habits or mindsets that make it easier for evangelical undergraduates to enact integrating approaches: identifying commonalities between themselves and non-evangelicals, and seeing their faith-based activism as about meeting material needs and not just evangelism or "culture wars" issues. She also writes that despite the possible and legitimate risks of inviting religious discourse into the composition classroom, they are necessary risks "if we truly want to support students' development of rhetorical skills and attitudes that contribute to civil discourse" (157). If writing teachers do not take up this challenge, we delegate evangelical students' rhetorical education exclusively to forces like the National Right to Life Commission. Cope also offers several practical ways for teachers to productively engage evangelical students, including assigning inquiry-oriented research and writing that will not allow them to recycle already-known research and talking points, and connecting the norms of academic writing to disciplinary goals and values.

Any acknowledgment of this book's broader value has to start by saying that I had already begun writing this book review when I got the news that Emily Cope had passed away very unexpectedly in the spring of this year; her students, colleagues, and extended community are grieving the loss of a teacher-scholar responsible for such fabulous work, work that addresses lots of my own curiosities and concerns about how (as a progressive, sometimes-visibly-queer religious person) I can interact productively with my evangelical undergraduates at the large southern public universities I've been teaching in for the past seven years (including the one at which, years apart, Cope and I both completed our doctoral research, which for her was the foundation of this project). I often find myself enacting compartmentalization in the classroom, sometimes speaking of my identities in ways that resonate—to use DePalma et al.'s term—with my Roman Catholic or Mormon students, and other times in ways that resonate with my queer religiously-deconstructed students. The work of integration is difficult, and requires time and attention to writing, to community, and to changing beliefs and values. In light of Cope's encouraging findings about how rhetorical education contributes to productive identity integration, I find that this text productively contributes to ongoing disciplinary conversations about the value of actually doing the writing and the research work yourself in the age of AI shortcuts. I am most encouraged, though, by how this research centers students' own explorations of their academic and evangelical lives. Despite researcher-led calls to reconsider queer and religious discourses in the classroom and public life (Cavallaro; Geiger), it hits different in 2025 to watch a young white cishet male student use multiple years of his academic research and writing to explore how his evangelical Christian identity compels him to figure out how to make the church less harmful and more welcoming to his queer neighbors.

Works Cited

Cavallaro, A. J. "Fighting Biblical 'Textual Harassment': Queer Rhetorical Pedagogies in the Extracurriculum." *Enculturation*, vol.18, 2015. http://enculturation.net/fighting-biblical-textual-harassment

DePalma, M.-J., P Lynch and J Ringer, editors. *Rhetoric and Religion in the Twenty-First Century: Pluralism in a Postsecular Age.* Southern Illinois University Press, 2023.

Dively, R. L. "Censoring Religious Rhetoric in the Composition Classroom: What We and Our Students May Be Missing." *Composition Studies*, vol. 25, no.1, 1997, pp. 55–66.

Geiger, T. "Emerging Voices: Unpredictable Encounters: Religious Discourse, Sexuality, and the Free Exercise of Rhetoric." *College English*, vol. 75, no. 3, 2013, pp 248–169.

Pugh, M. C. *An Investigation of Transfer in the Literacy Practices of Religiously Engaged Christian College Students,* 2015. University of Michigan, PhD dissertation. http://hdl.handle.net/2027/mdp.39015089719770

Rand, L. A. "Enacting faith: Evangelical discourse and the discipline of composition studies." *College Composition and Communication*, vol. 52, no. 3, 2001, pp. 349-367.

Ringer, J. M. *Vernacular Christian Rhetoric and Civil Discourse: The Religious Creativity of Evangelical Student Writers.* Routledge, 2016. http://ebookcentral.proquest.com/lib/bayloru/detail.action?docID=4391984

Ringer, J. M. "Working With(in) the Logic of the Jeremiad: Responding to the Writing of Evangelical Christian Students." *College Composition and Communication*, vol. 68, no. 4, 2017, pp. 629–654.

Thomson-Bunn, H. "Student Perspectives on Faith in the Classroom: Religious Discourses and Rhetorical Possibilities." *Pedagogy Critical Approaches to Teaching Literature Language Composition and Culture*, vol. 17, no. 3, 2017, pp. 373-396. https://doi.org/10.1215/15314200-3975447

Vander Lei, E. "Where the Wild Things Are: Christian Students in the Figured Worlds of Composition Research." *Mapping Christian Rhetorics: Connecting Conversations, Charting New Territories*, edited by Michael-John DePalma and Jeffrey M. Ringer, Routledge, 2014, pp. 65–85.

Poetter, Thomas S. *Curriculum Fragments: A Currere Journey Through Life Processes.* Routledge, 2025, 167 pages.

Joseph Wiederhold
Indiana University of Pennsylvania

> My intention isn't to create answers but to surface stories that lead to further questions, and to understanding perhaps. Maybe the stories will lead to new possibilities. Maybe they will lead to growth, and love. Ultimately, I am convinced that we are taught the things that distance us and connect us, subtly and not so subtly by the world, by our families, by our communities, by our experiences, and by our non-experiences. We all have our own stories to tell and to interrogate. I would like to hear more of them, not fewer of them, even the ugly ones. (Poetter 122)

Poetter's book *Curriculum Fragments*—and the stories shared within—have changed the way I think about education. Redefined it. Recentered it on what matters most—the human experience, the life processes at the center of Poetter's book: losing, knowing, forgiving, relating, hoping, growing, loving. Each of Poetter's fragments—reflective narratives written following the Currere methodology (Pinar)—caused me to reevaluate my practice. Here is one example from my own classroom of how a fragment from Poetter's book inspired me to recenter my practice:

"Talk to me about if or how you used AI to write this paper?"

"What?! I didn't use AI," my student replied.

"Okay, but just explain to me how you used it."

"I swear I didn't use AI. I wrote the paper myself."

"..."

"Okay, well, I mean, I guess I just asked it for some ideas, and then it gave me back, you know, some ideas, and I just copied and pasted those, but I changed some words around, so I still wrote it."

It was the end of the year, and this was the second time I had talked with this student about inappropriate usage of AI to complete coursework. I teach high school juniors, and this year was particularly rough. I love teaching, and I love my students, but I was at the point where I was turning towards cynicism. Giving up hope on having authentic learning experiences co-constructed between student and teacher, both invested in the betterment of our ability to think, communicate, and navigate our way through this world.

Poetter's book made its way to me during this low stretch of the school year, a time filled with makeup tests, plagiarism, and last-minute grade grubbing. In low moments like this, it's easy to see how education can be reduced to a transactional Freirean banking model: Tell me what I need to know. Tell me what I need to do to pass the class. To earn the grade. To check off the next box. And it would be easy to sentence my change-some-words-around student with a summary judgement of what I read from their behavior. But I realize after reading Poetter's book that both of those impulses are mutually—and needlessly—oppressive, placing student and teacher at odds with one another.

I felt this tension reflected early on in *Curriculum Fragments* when Poetter explores an early memory: during a one-on-one basketball game, young Poetter wrestles with a friend over a ball (45-50). I was struck by the poignant treatment of what seemed to me at first a fairly mundane, common interaction between two competitive boys. The story got me thinking about what might be happening within the interiority of my students' experience in my classroom. I thought about how I might be metaphorically wrestling with my student over a loose ball. The story gave me pause. Helped me realize that whatever I said and did with my AI-plagiarizing-student in such a crucial moment of vulnerability could potentially reverberate through their memory in the same way a simple moment in time still lived inside Poetter's memory.

So, with my student, rather than focusing on the behavior (AI plagiarism), or discipline, my brain began searching for generative ways forward, toward hope, and growth, and learning and at least understanding and forgiveness—all repeated themes in Poetter's work. My student and I had a good talk where I listened more than I talked, where my heart moved from cynicism to empathy for the situation. We made a plan together that ultimately led to some good writing (for both of us). We were both educated through the experience.

That clarity of focus on the human experience is the intention of *Curriculum Fragments*. Poetter's book isn't about AI, and that basketball memory isn't even explored or analyzed in the way I took it, and yet, the story helped me with my student because that was the problem I brought to my experience reading.

Intentionally or unintentionally, Poetter presents a metaphor for the potential of this type of personal meaning-making. In Poetter's first curriculum fragment, he writes about driving around a corner on a road he has driven many times. But because of the circumstances of that exact moment—the slant of light, the way the cars were arranged on the road—he was able to see something new. Something that was mundane and static was suddenly bursting with new life and insight (4-5). When I read Poetter's stories, they cast new rays of light on my experience, helping illuminate my thinking in exciting, inspiring new ways.

For this co-construction of knowledge, Poetter offers another metaphor of a kilonova (30-31)—a cosmic event where two bodies of dense matter collide, releasing new energy, elements (literally gold), and light. The metaphorical dense matter here being Poetter's Currere reflections colliding with the readers' questions, struggles and lived experience. The result, for me, was kilonova-explosive: rather than a static absorption of the author's ideas, I experienced a burst of insight and energy that reshaped how I think about education and life. That's a bold claim, I know, and not one I'd make lightly or universally. But for me—for my experience as a reader—that's exactly what this book did. Literally gold.

Structure of the Book

The book is organized into ten chapters, the first two devoted to establishing the conceptual framework necessary for making sense of the curriculum fragments that follow. Chapter One offers an overview of Louise Berman's life process–centered curriculum alongside Poetter's extensions and adaptations, particularly his integration of Pinar's Currere methodology: "the autobiographical, phenomenological, and psychoanalytic approach to curriculum studies" (8). Chapter Two offers the clearest and most thorough explanation of the Currere method I've read. Even though Poetter encourages readers to consult Pinar's original essay for a deeper understanding of Currere as a research tool, methodology, or reflective practice, I would actually recommend Poetter's Chapter Two as the most accessible resource. Poetter breaks down each step—regressive, progressive, synthetical—with more clarity and insight than Pinar's original essay.

And here comes a warning, the reader does need to invest in these initial chapters—into learning the rules of the game. The chapters are very readable, and Poetter does a good job weaving in some Currere reflections to model the process, as well as to start building the meaning for the work, but it is slightly akin to reading extensive rules before playing a new boardgame. But this is a game worth playing.

The next seven chapters provide the main organizing structure of Poetter's book, each centered on a core life process: losing, knowing, forgiving, relating, hoping, growing, loving. Each process is explored in its own chapter through stories accompanied by reflections, wonderings, possibilities, and implications. Reading these chapters feels a lot like settling into a warm dinner conversation: the kind you don't want to leave because of the comfort, the flow of ideas, and the ease of connection. And just as the feeling of an evening's conversation often lingers longer than the specific words exchanged, the same is true of this book.

Lest you think I am painting a rose-colored review, I must give a second warning or rather pass along and agree with Poetter's own warning: "I also want the reader to know that hoping to be understood, to understand myself, doesn't mean that everything here is tidy, neat, always well-packaged" (19). The stories read metaphorically, allegorically, and while that makes for powerful potential take-aways for the reader, it can also leave the reader reaching for meaning, feeling slightly disconnected from the intended meaning. Again, like a good dinner conversation, I didn't feel the need to fully interrogate every idea before me.

Poetter spends the final, very brief chapter tidying ideas up a bit, drawing a few more conclusions, explaining a bit more about his conceptualization for the book. We learn that he drew inspiration from Kierkegard's *Philosophical Fragments* which makes more sense in hindsight because the book does read closer to philosophical ponderings and introspection than a typical book on curriculum; however, Poetter is very clear that this isn't the book for a reader seeking a clearly defined curriculum; "instead, life processes constitute a valuable heuristic for getting at the nature and meaning, and possibly at the generative powers for thinking and practice that emerge from certain curriculum experiences . . ." (162).

Curriculum Fragments presents a challenge to review: it's not something easily explained or summarized. It needs to be experienced. I could tell you that this book inspired me. That it has illuminated anew the way I view myself as a teacher, the way I consider my students first as human beings, the way I think about my school and classroom and community and self, but that would be kind of like me trying to explain or describe the overwhelming feeling I experience witnessing the majesty of a perfect sunset. It would make more sense to invite you to come stand with me. To experience it—read it—for yourself.

Works Cited

Berman, L. M. *New Priorities in the Curriculum*. Charles E Merrill Publishing Company, 1968.
Freire, P. *Pedagogy of the Oppressed*. Continuum, 2018. (Original work published 1968).
Kierkegaard, S. *Philosophical fragments/Johannes Climacus*. Translated by H. V. Hong & E. H. Hong, Princeton University Press, 1985.
Pinar, W. *Autobiography, Politics, and Sexuality: Essays in Curriculum Theory, 1972-199*. Peter Lang, 1994.

Williams, Bronwyn T. *Literacies in Times of Disruption: Living and Learning During a Pandemic.* Routledge, 2024, 238 pages.

Ashna Singh
Miami University of Ohio

This review is structured around three central concepts that Williams develops throughout this book: affect, assemblages, and the connection between memory and identity. In *Literacies in Times of Disruption: Living and Learning During a Pandemic*, Williams focuses on the narratives of over thirty university students at the University of Louisville to examine how their literacy practices and emerging identities were influenced by physical, emotional, and structural crises. He explores how overlapping disruptions such as the COVID-19 pandemic, racial violence and police brutality in the wake of George Floyd and Breonna Taylor's murders, and mounting environmental threats deeply affected students' literate lives. Additionally, he emphasizes how shifting material conditions and emotionally charged home-school settings altered their literate identities.

Williams frames his interpretation of students' narrative entanglements over the two-year study by building on theories of affect, emotion, and memory and analyzing their experiences with literacy instruction and digital media through the lens of "sociomaterial uses of assemblages" (14). In part, their relationships with instructors and institutions evolved accordingly. He argues that students' literate lives are inseparable from the emotional and material conditions of these crises. More importantly, we must play the *believing game* instead of the *doubting game* with the lived experiences of students (Elbow). A central insight Williams offers is that emotion is not separate from learning; it saturates *every* aspect of it. He draws on affect theory to show how emotional responses are not incidental to literacy development but firmly rooted within it. Many students reported cognitive overload caused by the constant stress and trauma of the pandemic—from anxiety and anger to burnout and disillusionment. This disruption fundamentally impacted their ability to focus and engage in academic work. These turned out to be normal and appropriate responses to extraordinary, traumatic conditions, rather than individual shortcomings or learning deficits (81).

According to Williams' findings, the blurring of boundaries between home and school spaces intensified feelings of exhaustion and burnout, particularly as students struggled to maintain academic motivation in environments filled with personal and societal stressors. Furthermore, Williams defines affective responses as emotional reactions that are embodied and often felt before they can be fully recognized or articulated cognitively (11). These affective responses shape more than day-to-day motivation—it fundamentally influences students' cognition, agency, and identities as learners and writers. Students' feelings of shame, guilt, and self-blame when struggling with reading and writing practices often collided internally with new pandemic traumas (40-42). Rather than viewing these struggles as personal deficiencies, Williams situates them within the broader material and emotional stressors of the pandemic.

In *Literacies*, he challenges traditional binaries between home and school, arguing that the pandemic revealed the inadequacy of thinking about learning spaces as fixed or stable. Instead, students' experiences illustrated that spaces are dynamic "assemblages" (Deleuze and Guattari)--ever-shifting intersections of material conditions, emotional states, cultural narratives, and literacy practices (131). As a result, students reimagined their environments in response to pandemic demands: transforming bedrooms, kitchen tables, parking lots, and other nontraditional physical and virtual spaces into sites of learning and writing. These assemblages of space were not simply temporary adaptations; they became vital ecosystems where students negotiated their literate and emotional lives. Throughout his study, Williams observes how students developed new concepts of comfort and efficiency within these assemblages–reshaping their relationships to space, technology, and learning routines.

As students adapted to new learning spaces, they were also actively reconstructing their memories and identities, weaving together the past, present, and future. Williams challenges the notion of memory as a static archive that simply preserves past experiences. By drawing on theories of autobiographical memory, he frames memory as a fluid and ongoing process–continually shaped by students' current emotions, needs, and imagined futures (82, 90). Many students revised memories of disruption, trauma, resilience, and adaptation in order to make sense of who they were during the pandemic and who they would become (131, 136). These were not passive recollections but active, meaningful acts that shaped how students understood themselves as learners and writers. Williams pinpoints the complexity of this process, noting that memory and narrative often clash–moments of pride existing alongside feelings of failure or shame. These tensions, he argues, are not inconsistencies but markers of lived reality: "Memory is an artist as much as it's a scientist" (90). Crucially, Williams asserts that the emotional dispositions formed during this time will endure, guiding how students respond to future educational challenges and possibilities.

However, students did not face challenges solely on an individual level; they experienced ambiguous loss and emotional blending across personal, academic, and social domains. Williams illustrates how the loss of once-anticipated milestones clashed with the weight of social and political anxieties and personal traumas. Additionally, his analysis of the pandemic reveals the neoliberal ideologies that increasingly govern universities. Students in Williams' study articulated a growing sense of betrayal and disillusionment as they observed university administrations emphasizing enrollment numbers, tuition revenues, and public image while neglecting the physical, emotional, and material needs of their student populations (76). This loss of trust is not a temporary sentiment, Williams cautions, but a significant wound that will have lasting consequences for how students relate to institutions of higher learning. Williams raises concerns about the long-term effects of student skepticism: can universities genuinely rebuild trust, or will they continue to uphold structures that alienate those they claim to serve? (220).

Toward the end of *Literacies*, Williams proposes a call-to-action for educators and institutions: we must not merely aim to return to the pre-pandemic "normal." Instead, he pushes us to reclaim "enchantment" and revive "vitality" in education, recognizing that learning is deeply affective, embodied, and relational (213, 218). The future of education needs more than just technological adjustment. Williams argues that pedagogy must address the emotional, material, and imaginative dimensions of learning that the pandemic so vividly exposed. As students reshaped their physical and digital spaces during the pandemic, they demonstrated how learning is never disembodied: it is always tied to external and internal forces. Williams calls on educators to center these realities–designing pedagogical spaces that are attentive to the ways time, place, memory, emotion, and social connection shape students' literate lives. Williams reminds us that "these disruptions will continue to affect students' lives, our culture, and the affective and embodied responses in the classroom" (221). Therefore, this is not a moment for nostalgia, despair, or retreat, but an opportunity to disrupt the world around us in pursuit of more liberating forms of education. The pandemic drastically unveiled an educational system that may no longer meet many students' needs. In *Literacies*, Williams binds together shared stories of loss, adaptation, and resilience. At the heart of it, he calls on educators, researchers, writing and media studies specialists to recognize and nurture the humanity in one another and our students. Consequently, we can continuously (re)create these spaces together for years to come.

Works Cited

Elbow, P. (2008). "The Believing Game or Methodological Believing." *JAEPL*, vol.14, pp. 1-11.

Contributors to JAEPL, Vol. 30

Janelle Adsit is an Associate Professor of English at Cal Poly Humboldt in northern California. Janelle has authored, co-authored, and edited books for teachers of creative writing, along with recent books on the environmental humanities (Routledge, 2021) and narrative medicine (Bloomsbury Academic, 2025). ja2828@humboldt.edu

Bhushan Aryal is an Associate Professor of English and Director of the Composition and Speech Program at Delaware State University. Originally from the hills of Lumbini Province in Nepal—birthplace of Siddhartha Gautama—Bhushan observes that one of his current wonders has been how his ancient villager has become a ubiquitous modern icon, appearing everywhere from meditation retreats to the "Buddha statues" in Western supermarkets. baryal@desu.edu

Beverly Brannan teaches in the English Department at the University of Cincinnati. During her twenty-five years of teaching, she has taught a wide variety of classes for the English Composition program. Many of the classes are focused on community, identity, and culture, and are often interactive classes. She recently designed a new class, Life, Happiness, and Resilience, to assist students in reducing their stress and anxiety, and to help them learn how to be happier in life. beverly.brannan@uc.edu

Geraldine DeLuca is the author of *Bensonhurst Sutra: Tales of an Italian American Buddhist*, December 2024. In 2018, she published *Teaching Toward Freedom: Voices and Silence in the English Classroom* (Routledge). She also co-founded and for many years co-edited a journal about children's book entitled *The Lion and the Unicorn*. It is now published by Johns Hopkins UP. Her website is GeraldineDeLuca.com. She is professor emerita of English at Brooklyn College, CUNY, where, for many years, she was Director of Freshman English and Coordinator of Writing Across the Curriculum. She chaired the Advisory Committee of AEPL for three years and was grateful for the opportunity to work with its vibrant board. She is also happy to let go and watch it flourish under its current wonderful leadership! gerideluca228@gmail.com

Sue Doe teaches courses in Composition, Autoethnographic Theory and Method, Reading and Writing Connections, Research Methods, and GTA preparation for writing instruction. She does research in three distinct areas--academic labor and the faculty career, writing across the curriculum, and student-veteran transition in the post-9/11 era. Coauthor of the faculty development book Concepts and Choices: Meeting the Challenges in Higher Education, she has published articles in College English, The WAC Journal, Reflections, and Writing Program

Administration (among others) as well as in several book-length collections. Her collection on student-veterans in the Composition classroom, Generation Vet: Composition, Veterans, and the Post-911 University, co-edited with Professor Lisa Langstraat, was published by Utah State Press (an imprint of the University Press of Colorado) in 2014. From 2020-2023 Sue focused on leading faculty participation in shared governance while serving as Chair of the Faculty Council. Currently she serves as Executive Director of The Institute for Learning and Teaching. Sue's scholarship has followed this direction, looking at leadership responsibility for the empowerment and valuing of writing instruction and the broader educational mission of colleges and universities. sue.doe@colostate.edu

Matthew Lemas is a lecturer in rhetoric and composition at Chapman University in Southern California. His pedagogical interests include the application of mindfulness concepts and practices to the writing process, as well as, more broadly, student well-being. mlemas@chapman.edu

Marian Mesrobian MacCurdy, retired professor and chair of the Department of Writing at Ithaca College is the author of several books and many articles the former including The Mind's Eye: Image and Memory in Writing about Trauma, Sacred Justice: the Voices and Legacy of the Armenian Operation Nemesis, and Writing and Healing: Toward an Informed Practice (co-edited with Charles Anderson). She has taught at Colgate University, Hampshire College, and most recently the University of Massachusetts. maccurdy@ithaca.edu

Nate Mickelson teaches undergraduate writing at NYU, where he also helps coordinate the writing program. He is working on a study of «small aesthetics,» or experiences of interpretation and critical care elicited by contemporary poetry and visual art. In collaboration with colleagues, he has published research on contract grading, classroom community agreements, learning communities, and outcomes assessment. Nate currently chairs AEPL›s Executive Committee and has been co-organizer of one in-person AEPL conference, 2017, «Writing as a Way of Being Human,» and two online conferences, 2020, «Humanizing Online Teaching,» and 2024, «Enacting Empathy in the Classroom and Beyond.» mickelsonjn@gmail.com

Laurence Musgrove teaches literature, creative writing, and composition at Angelo State University in San Angelo, Texas. His poetry collections include *The Bluebonnet Sutras, A Stranger's Heart,* and *The Dogs of Alishan and Other Poems from Taiwan.* He cartoons at texosophy.substack.com. lmusgrove@angelo.edu

Irene Papoulis is the author of a textbook, *The Essays Only You Can Write,* (Broadview Press, 2023.) She recently retired from teaching at Trinity College,

Hartford, and is a former AEPL co-chair, with Wendy Ryden. Irene.Papoulis@trincoll.edu

Kristin Bryant Rajan, Ph.D. in English, writes poetry, fiction, creative nonfiction, and literary criticism in Atlanta, GA and is a senior lecturer in English at Kennesaw State University. Her work—centered on themes of healing and wellbeing, sometimes with a dash of humor—appears in a range of creative and academic journals, anthologies, and edited collections. She is a *Best of the Net*, the *Pushcart Prize*, and *Georgia Author of the Year* nominee. Her poetry chapbook, *Shadows*, was published in 2024, Finishing Line Press. When not writing or teaching, she leads some lively Spin classes at the Decatur YMCA. You can find her published work and curated playlists at kristinrajan.com. kristinbryantrajan@gmail.com

Sarah Robinson graduated from University of Massachusetts Amherst cum laude with a Bachelors in English and with greatest distinction from the Honors College. She is currently persuing her Masters in Elementary Education at Merrimack College. Sarah lives with her partner of 6 years and their rescue dog Onyx in the Pioneer Valley. sarahrobinson.se@gmail.com

Kris Saknussemm is a multimedia artist, musician, and the author of a range of books including his latest work *A Guide to Creative Writing and the Imagination* published by Routledge Press. He received a B.A. with Distinction from Dartmouth, double majoring in English and Native American Studies and holds an M.A. from the University of Washington where he was the Robertson Fellow. His first novel *Zanesville* was nominated for the Philip K. Dick Award and became a cult favorite in translation in Russia and Poland. His novel *Private Midnight* achieved bestseller status in France and Italy. His work *The Memory Wound* won First Prize in the *Missouri Review* Audio Play competition, and the film of his published play *The Humble Assessment* (which was the featured work at the Las Vegas Fringe Festival and has also been staged in Australia and Sweden) has been screened at 19 international festivals. He has been a Fellow at MacDowell and the Black Mountain Institute, Distinguished Artist in Residence at Seattle University, Visiting Master Artist at Salem State University and California State University Dominguez Hills, and a Mellon Scholar in Residence at Rhodes University in South Africa. After living half his life outside America, he lives now in Boulder City, Nevada and is currently an Adjunct Professor at UNLV.

Kelly Morgan Sauskojus is a Postdoctoral Fellow at Clemson University with interests in religious rhetorics and community organizing. They contribute to local food justice movements (growing food, teaching classes, and researching and writing grants) and were interviewed by NPR's All Things Considered for how such work creates alternative spiritual communities. ksausko@clemson.edu

Ashna Singh is currently a PhD student in Composition and Rhetoric at Miami University. Her research explores contemplative pedagogy, literacy studies, and cultural rhetorics. She enjoys collecting vinyl records, painting, and making digital collages. singha37@miamioh.edu

Joseph Wiederhold has taught English Language Arts for fifteen years. He currently teaches at Provo High School and is working toward a PhD in Composition and Applied Linguistics at Indiana University of Pennsylvania. He is passionate about writing instruction and working with teachers as an associate director of the Central Utah Writing Project. wzrdc@iup.edu

Dr. Adrian Matt Zytkoskee has been teaching writing in higher education and community settings for eighteen years and is currently an assistant professor of English at the American University of Sharjah, UAE. His research focuses upon narrative medicine in healthcare settings, narrative scholarship, writing and healing, communication in grief, life writing, group facilitation, and effective feedback practices. His mission for this work is to help people process, navigate, and document human experiences through writing. He is also an avid musician and a grateful father of two beautiful children. azytkoskee@aus.edu

PARLOR PRESS
EQUIPMENT FOR LIVING

Now with Parlor Press!

Studies in Rhetorics and Feminism
  New Series Editors: Jessica Enoch and Sharon Yam

Critical Conversations in Higher Education Leadership
  Series Editor: Victor E. Taylor

New Releases

Plato's Nightmare by Steven B. Katz

The SoTL Guide: (Re)Orienting the Scholarship of Teaching and Learning by Nancy L. Chick, Peter Felten, and Katarina Mårtensson

Storied Objects: A Graphic Narrative Reflection on Material Metaphors and Digital Writing by Erin Kathleen Bahl

Xeno >> Glossia: An Illuminated Study of Christine de Pizan by Marci Vogel

Rhetorical Reception: One Hundred and Fifty Years of Arguing with Sex in Education by Carolyn Skinner

City Housekeeping: Women's Labor Rhetorics and Spaces for Solidarity, 1886–1911 by Liane Malinowski

Kenneth Burke's Rhetoric of Identification by Tilly Warnock

Forthcoming in 2026

Shaping Rhetorical Studies: The Research of RSA Fellows, with Commentary edited by Cheryl Glenn and Richard Leo Enos

Teaching and Learning with Rhetorical Listening: Alternatives to Self-Censorship and Silence in High School and College Classrooms edited by Krista Ratcliffe and Jessica Rivera-Mueller

Check Out Our Website!

Discounts, blog, open access titles, instant downloads, and more.

parlorpress.com

JAEPL **Discount:** Use JAEPL20 at checkout to receive a 20% discount on all titles not on sale through January 1, 2026.

www.ingramcontent.com/pod-product-compliance
Lightning Source LLC
Chambersburg PA
CBHW021950160426
43195CB00011B/1302